AUSTRALIAN RAILWAYS

AUSTRALIAN RAILWAYS

Their Life and Times

Robin Bromby

Highgate Publishing

Based on *The Railway Age in Australia* and *Ghost Railways of Australia* published by Lothian Books in 2004 and 2005 respectively along with new, additional material.

This collected edition published 2013 by
Highgate Publishing.
PO Box 481
Edgecliff NSW 2027
Australia

Email: info@highgatepublishing.com.au

ISBN: 978-0-9874038-6-5

www.highgatepublishing.com.au

Cover: A 1968 scene as Victorian Railways locomotive B 65 hauls a Melbourne-Ballarat passenger train. This scene, near the town of Bacchus Marsh, no longer exists: the trestle bridge is gone, the area beneath it having been filled in. (*Roy Sinclair*)

Contents

Introduction

'Railroading is only ten per cent iron;
the other ninety per cent are men.'

- Legendary Victorian Railway Commissioner Harold Clapp
heard this from the President of Southern Pacific Railroad,
and made it his motto

WHEN THE NEW SOUTH WALES mining town of Cobar in 1992 celebrated the centenary of its connection to the railway network, a local historian recalled how the daily train departure to Sydney had once been the big event of the day. Around the start of the First World War, women would come to the station to farewell friends; they would be dressed in tailored suits, their hair done up in a bun, both hair and hat kept in place by several long pins. Veils and gloves would always have been worn. Shopkeepers armed with warrants would be watching to see whether any of their debtors were skipping town; if so, they could call the police-man who always attended the daily departure.

Children returning to boarding school would be neatly dressed, complete with school ties. Commercial travellers would be boarding with their sample cases, having filled their order books to be taken back to Sydney. Local businessmen needing to have meetings in the big smoke would join the train, too. The guard's van, placed opposite the parcels office, would be in the process of being loaded, the huge steel trunks belonging to passengers being heaved aboard. Portmanteaux and Gladstone bags would be taken inside the carriages by the travellers and placed in the luggage racks. The guard's van included a travelling post office, and letters could be posted through a slot in the side of the van right up until the train departed.

Welcome to the age when the railway was part of almost every Australian's life. Even if they did not travel on trains all that often, the average Australian would have got most of the necessities of life via the railway. For those boarding our train at Cobar, the trip would be twenty hours, complete with refreshment stops at Nyngan, Wellington and Orange. But that twenty hours was a good deal better than the week it would have taken to cover the same distance by horse-drawn vehicle.

*   *   *

The term 'railway age' can be defined in many ways. At its broadest, it could span the nearly 160 years from the first steam-hauled journey in Melbourne on 13 September 1854 to the present day. After all, the completion of the transcontinental line to Darwin in 2003, along with the subsequent introduction of the Tilt Train in Queensland, demonstrate that railways are, in one sense, even now renewing themselves. New suburban lines have followed the ever increasing city extremities. Intermodal freight is light years from the 'stop and shunt at every station' goods (or freight) trains of a now departed era.

Fifty or more years ago, many Australians would have seen trains as part of their lives: they could usually see wagons left at their local country station siding either to have their loads of fertiliser collected by farmers or be stacked with wool bales bound for the sales; or they might be going down to that same small station to catch a railmotor or a slow, mixed (freight and passenger) train to the nearest mainline terminus, there to board an express for the big city. Or they might have worked for the railways; some centres employed hundreds, even thousands, of men and women to keep the trains rolling.

And railways were a part of life in the sense that so many knew someone who worked on the railways, or had a relation employed there. Scratch a third or more generation Australian, and the chances are that their grandfather, or great-uncle, was a driver here or a stationmaster there. Chris Holley, who spent most of his working life at Werris Creek, the important junction in northern New South Wales, had a father who was an engine driver. His two brothers were also employed by the railways, one as a fitter and turner, the other a locomotive engineman's timekeeper. His daughter was a clerk at Werris Creek, his son-in-law became an engine driver and his brother-in-law was the yard controller at the huge Enfield marshalling yards in Sydney. There are thousands of families with stories like this.

Much of that era has gone and, with it, what might be called the 'railway age'. Yet, even as late as Easter 1974, people still turned to rail in surprising numbers. Normally, the one overnight Vinelander service was sufficient for people wanting to travel from Melbourne to Mildura on the Victoria-New South Wales border. But on Good Friday 1974, such was the demand, Victorian

Railways announced there would be three trains that night going north-west. It was still not enough; a fourth train was added at the last moment, and between them the trains carried sixty-five cars on motorail wagons. They were scheduled to pull out of Melbourne at 8.20 pm, 9.05 pm, 9.30 pm and 10.30 pm. Even though the stationmaster at Mildura had organised to have the yard as free as possible of goods wagons, the passenger movements put great strain on the station facilities, the last train having to wait at Irymple, 6 km from Mildura, until the preceding consists could be moved to sidings and the platform line cleared.

Another definition of the 'railway age' could see it as spanning from 1874 until 1920, the years that saw the greatest burst of railway construction and the completion of most of the main lines of the national network, including the long steel road across the 2,000 km-wide treeless Nullarbor Plain that separates Western Australia from the east of the island continent. Yet even that is not entirely satisfactory as a definition. For example, in the 1950s, Victorian Railways ordered new fleets of railmotors for country lines because, even then, many rural people were without their own motorcar. In 1955, Victorian Railways had 838 railway stations open to traffic; fully 633 of those were served by passenger trains. It was in the 1950s, too, that Victorian Railways launched its Operation Phoenix under which £80 million — no small sum back then — was earmarked for the upgrading and modernising of its system.

At its zenith, the governmental railway system in Australia reached a length of 44,344 route kilometres.

This book is an attempt to capture how it was back then. Before it began to shrink and change and never be the same again.

*   *   *

The Australian railways were a place where, once you got a job with all the security that entailed, people tended to stay for life. And the job stayed in the family. Alfred Vivian Green was just such an example.

Born in 1875, he was just six years old when his father, a locomotive driver, was killed in a shunting accident at Gerogery, north of Albury, New South Wales. And Alfred had two younger sisters. By the time he turned fifteen years of age, Alfred had resolved to devote himself to supporting his mother — who had kept some money coming in by working at the railway refreshment rooms — and two siblings for as long as needed; when he reached that age of fifteen, he was given a job as a junior porter with New South Wales Government Railways (NSWGR). Alfred's subsequent career with NSWGR included a stint at the Eveleigh railway workshops in Sydney but he worked the trains, too, rising to the level of fireman. By the time his mother died, Alfred's life pattern was formed. His filial devotion had deprived him of the opportunity of marriage and a family of his own.

Instead, in his later years, he devoted himself to the enthusiast movement. He compiled a reference book listing the details of every steam locomotive used in the railway systems of New South Wales and Victoria; he also committed to memory all the road numberings, re-numberings and builders' plate numberings for every steam locomotive used in every state in Australia (bar one) and New Zealand. He was known for his ability to reproduce vocally the sounds of various pieces of railway equipment in use. For Alfred Green, as for so many of his generation, working in the railways was a way of life.

When the New South Wales railway system in September 2005 celebrated its 150th year of existence, the government railways were surpassed in longevity by one family which had helped build the first line in the state.

John Doggett, from Waterbeach near Cambridge in England, arrived in the colony in 1853, one of the five hundred navvies recruited to lay the rail line between what is now Redfern (in inner Sydney) and Parramatta. This line opened in September 1855. Two of the other navvies were his sons, Charles and William. There was also Mary, his wife, and a daughter, Eliza, who had arrived on the vessel *David McIvor*.

In 1854, John's son William married another Eliza, this one from County Kildare in Ireland. William was eventually employed as a ganger at Petersham (now another inner suburb of Sydney) at the wage of eight shillings and sixpence a day, while his wife became gatekeeper at the station, being on hand to close off the roadway at the level crossing whenever a train approached. She added ten shillings a week to the family budget. They would serve at many stations in New South Wales: William put in forty-six years for the railway, while Eliza did forty years as a gatekeeper.

Of the eight children born to William and Eliza, all six sons joined the NSWGR. William Junior served for thirty-five years, Henry joined in 1878 as a plumber boy on three shillings and sixpence a day, John spent thirty-one years on the railways and ended his career at Mudgee station, James put in forty-nine years (and his wife, Sarah, did thirteen years as a gatekeeper), George was employed by the railway for forty-five years and Charles ended up as a stationmaster (at Crookwell). The two daughters married railway men. Mary Ann wed James Piggott, a block layer, while Emily married George Featherstone, who would rise to the rank of engine driver.

And so it went on through the generations. In 2005, Doggett family descendants were still employed in the state's railway system.

One was a signal electrician, another a train controller; there were also Doggett family members working as a statistician for the railways, a duty manager, a driver-in-training, a safety co-ordinator, another in incident manager and one as a rail vehicle body builder.

Outside of the cities, people depended on their railways — and the people who served in them. Take the Injune branch in Queensland that ran out in the countryside from the rail junction at Roma: the regular guard in the 1930s, Ken Bell, would look after all the shopping at Hunters store in Roma, with women all along the branch giving him their shopping lists. When personal items were required, Bell would ask the lady concerned to place the details in an envelope that he could hand over to the store. On the return journey to Injune, the guard would disperse the wrapped and addressed parcels. As this was the time before Injune had a pub — the line ran through several soldier settlements and these areas were not allowed to have a hotel for the first fifteen years of their existence — Bell would hide all the beer and other liquor bought in Roma beneath the coal in the tender (just in case the coppers were around) and then deliver orders to the thirsty farmers.

One of the last guards working on the line, Johnny Russell, never needed the shopping lists. He had an amazing memory for all the detailed orders to be lodged with Hunters; he would even memorise the colour numbers for reels of cotton.

It was not just the country folk who felt the railways to be part of their lives. Stan Gratte became an engine driver in West Australian Government Railways at the unusually young age of twenty-four — he had joined in 1947 as an engine cleaner but rose quickly in a service which had lost many experienced men during the war. He recalled for the author that the twice-weekly passenger train from Geraldton to Perth always drew a crowd. Apart from those seeing off friends and relatives, many a Geraldton resident would wander down to the station just to watch all the activity of the train getting ready for departure. Again, railways in Western Australia were family affairs, too: Stan's cousin started as a call-boy — he delivered roster instructions to the homes of drivers, firemen and guards — and rose to head the state's railway department.

The steam engines have gone; the small rural stations with their goods sheds and sidings have gone; the branch line railmotor and mixed trains have all gone. This book is about serving their memory.

1

Heyday

PICTURE A SMALL WAYSIDE country station. It is unmanned but there is a siding with a few empty four-wheeled wagons; these may have brought bagged fertiliser for local farmers, or they may be left there for a farmer to load bales of wool or bags of wheat. On the platform sit cream cans — full, as it happens — so there must be a train due to collect them and cart them off to the nearest butter factory. Until that train arrives, there will be hardly a sound apart from the wind in the trees behind the station. Then, eventually, we hear the train approaching; it glides to a halt, the cream cans are rolled into the van, the van doors are slammed shut, the locomotive whistle is heard, and the train is on its way again. Within a few minutes, the place is once more silent.

This could have been any one of hundreds of places, fifty to a hundred years ago.

Picture, now, a station at a substantial regional centre. Take Mount Gambier in South Australia as a typical example. This station had become a very busy one when it was connected both to Wolseley to the north (on the South Australia system) and eastwards across the border to link up at Heywood with the Victorian Railways' Portland line. There were two yards at Mount Gambier, known respectively as the 'old' and the 'new'. The rails linking these two yards crossed two streets and the frequent disruption to traffic was a sore point with the locals; the engine crews knew to expect verbal complaints every time they shunted between the yards. Goods trains were assembled each day to run to Mile End yards in Adelaide and to the wharves at Portland across the border. Other traffic originating at Mount Gambier each day were the freight trains to Heywood and the overnight Blue Lake, the passenger service to Adelaide.

How New South Wales trains looked in the early years of the twentieth century. The 2-6-0 B 205-class locomotive No. 207 was released to traffic in 1882 and withdrawn in 1931. Its train consists of three F timber wagons, two D open wagons, one S steel-made open wagon, two CV vans, one end-platform suburban car, one Redfern car and a guard's van. Paddy Norton collection.

Mount Gambier had plenty of railway 'furniture': turntables, semaphore signals, water vats, coal stages and a locomotive depot where steam engines stood hissing in the sun between jobs. There were men toiling in the rail yard, passengers waiting to depart or friends and relatives standing on the platform awaiting to meet someone of an arriving train. These scenes have largely faded, and disappeared. As have many others.

*   *   *

The locomotive depot

Engine driver Jim Seletto was both a railwayman and a rail enthusiast. He also had the ability to set down memorable accounts for fellow enthusiasts of what he had seen at work. Of the North Melbourne locomotive depot, known in the 1950s and 1960s as 'the big smoke', he watched the lighters-up at work

> … each tending a dozen or more locomotives who were in the habit of going around their charges about half an hour before knock-off time and putting on a big fire in each locomotive, so that each relief man would have time for a cup of tea before tending what was now his charge. So that regularly at 6.30 am, 2.30 pm and 10.30 pm something like 200 hundred locomotives would receive twenty shovels of coal and then have the blowers shut off. Consequently, as can be imagined, a great deal of smoke would be given off at these times and thus the depot was known by one of its products.

Serving Spencer Street station and Melbourne's main freight yards, North Melbourne depot in the 1950s was a place of noise and smoke as engines arrived, were stabled and later readied for their next duty. The coal stage could, at any one time, handle three large locomotives of the X Class size, or five tank engines. Three tons of coal could be discharged into a tender in as many seconds; the water cranes could fill a large locomotive's tank in three minutes. Until 1960, the main pit could turn out a locomotive fully watered, coaled and sanded every five minutes. This capacity served the depot well on Christmas Eve 1954. Seventy trains were scheduled to depart from Spencer Street between 2.00 pm and 7.00 pm, and locomotives had to be provided without depriving freight workings of their needed motive power.

By 9.00 am that morning, the shed staff workers had chalked both sides of every locomotive cab with that train's destination and departure time. By 1.00 pm the first locomotive crews were clocking on. By 3.00 pm, as Seletto recorded it, all was noise, heat and confusion. Fitters were attending to any last minute locomotive problem while crews were either oiling their charges, washing cab windows or drinking tea. There was steam and smoke everywhere.

> Suddenly, an engine would whistle for the turntable, a score of watches would be scanned and the great parade would commence. Steam would scream out of a safety valve, usually scaring the crew oiling the engine alongside, then slowly and majestically an engine would move, steam spurting over the shed floor from its open cylinder drain cocks.

Shunters and crews of engines already in the yard would pause to watch the procession. As the last locomotive was dispatched, the shed staff could relax and have their next cup of tea. By 8.00 pm activity was building again as locomotives off country arrivals would start moving into the depot.

Workers at the Peterborough, South Australia, loco depot in 1920.
John Mannion Collection.

A busy evening at Sydney Steam Station

During the afternoon on a typical weekday in the 1950s, the staff at what was then called Sydney Steam Station (now generally known just as 'Central') would be kept busy by the steam-hauled departures of commuter trains to the outer areas of the metropolis such as Campbelltown and Liverpool. Although some would run into the evening, after peak-hour Sydney Steam Station became the preserve of the long distance trains. Passengers would arrive with suitcases rather than, as was the case a few hours earlier, briefcases. The ones with suitcases mostly faced all-night journeys. They would be buying magazines and newspapers for the long journey ahead; the station staff would help direct them to the right platform. The steam locomotives at the head of the trains would be quietly hissing, the firemen checking their gauges and the drivers waiting for the all-clear.

The evening departures had little to do with the needs of the passengers; they were, instead, timed to fit in with the requirements of the postal system, hence the word 'Mail' in the names of many of these trains. The mail collected in Sydney during the day and sorted would then be transported overnight by trains to destinations all over New South Wales and interstate.

The passengers would have to study their timetables if they were going to other than the more important destinations due to the fact that some services ran only on certain days of the week, and connecting services varied according to the day of the week. Those timetables, as the ones applying on 23 November 1952, meant that by 7.00 pm the concourse would be seeing the first of these long-distance travellers. The business of the evening at Sydney Steam Station began with the 7.25 pm departure for Coonamble, a town in the west of New South Wales. That train would travel on the Main West line as far as Dubbo, then turn off on to the Coonamble branch (which saw passenger services survive until the 1970s).

Another Sydney departure as 3801 is sending out smoke and steam as it takes up the weight of the passenger cars behind. This was taken at 9.00 am and the long-distance passenger platforms would have been comparatively quiet, the main express trains having arrived over preceding hours and the outward rush of passengers not due to start again until 7.00 pm. State Records NSW.

The timetable read:

7.25 pm: Coonamble via Lithgow. MONS and WEDS —
Connecting services Dubbo to Parkes and Warren. MONS —
Connecting service Dubbo-Bourke. WEDS —Connecting service
Dubbo-Cobar.

7.30 pm: Albury, change for Victorian stations. MONS and WEDS
— connecting train on Corowa line.

7.40 pm: South Brisbane.

8.03 pm: Murwillumbah; first stop Coffs Harbour.

8.10 pm: Victorian stations.

8.15 pm: MONS and WEDS — Murwillumbah, stopping
Broadmeadow, Dungog, Gloucester, etc. Connecting service
Casino-Cougar [a station on the North Coast Line just south of
the Queensland border]. TUES and THURS. First stop Kempsey.
Connecting services Casino-Cougar, Dorrigo branch. FRI — First
stop Coffs Harbour.

8.20 pm: TUES, THURS, FRI — Wyalong Central. Connecting
services to Yass Town, King's Vale to Blayney, Grenfell line,
Stockinbingal to Forbes, Pucawan to Griffith.
TUES and THURS — Train runs West Wyalong to Lake Cargelligo.
THURS — Connecting services on Rankins Springs and Naradhan
branch lines. THURS and FRI — Connecting service stopping
Tharbogang to Hillston.

8.30 pm: Forbes. Connecting services to Stockinbingal, Parkes-
Narromine, Condobolin, Molong-Dubbo. TUES and THURS
— Connecting services to Broken Hill, first stop Micabil. TUES —
Connecting services to Lowlands, Hillston. WEDS — Connecting
services Blayney-Cowra, Eugowra and Grenfell lines. TUES-FRI
— Connecting train to Tottenham branch.

8.58 pm: TUES, THURS and FRI — Bombala via Canberra. WEDS Cooma via Canberra.

9.03 pm: TUES, THURS, FRI — Kempsey. Change at Waratah for Sandgate, Victoria Street, High Street.

9.20 pm: TUES–FRI — Glen Innes. Connecting service Barraba line. TUES and THURS — Connecting service Werris Creek–Binnaway.

9.25 pm: TUES, THURS, FRI — Bourke. Connecting services Narromine–Parkes,

Nevertire–Warren. TUES and THURS — Connecting services Byrock–Brewarrina, Nyngan, Cobar, Dubbo to Merrygoen-Gwabegar and Binnaway–Werris Creek.

9.30 pm: Cowra. Connecting services Eugowra and Grenfell lines.

10.05 pm: MONS and WEDS — Griffith via Junee. Connecting services Murrumburrah to Young, Cootamundra West to Forbes, on Tocumwal line, Junee to Wagga Wagga, Griffith to Hay. WEDS — Connecting services on Boorowa line, Wagga Wagga to The Rock. TUES, THURS and FRI — Connecting services on Tumut and Batlow branch lines, Tocumwal line. TUES and THURS — Connecting service to Hay.

10.30 pm: TUES, THURS and FRI — Albury, change for Victorian stations. Connecting services to Young, Tumbarumba branch, The Rock to Urana. FRI — Connecting service Boorowa branch. TUES and THURS — Connecting services Crookwell and Oaklands branches. THURS — Connecting train Corowa line. FRI — Connecting service Henty to Rand.

*　　*　　*

In 1929 ticket collector 'Johnson' penned this impression of his workplace, Sydney Steam Stations's main terminal.

THE PASSING SHOW

I had wandered, rather slowly,
In and out amongst the crowd,
That had gathered on the concourse,
Where the paper boys aloud,
Roar out: A bun or a snooze, sir?
How the people rush and go,
So I stood for half an hour,
And surveyed the passing show.

There a mother and her kiddies,
With her husband long and lean,
Taking holidays in Sydney,
From the bush, that's easily seen.
He's a drover down from Warren,
Where the dusty winds do blow,
And I thought of sheep and gum trees,
As I watched the passing show.

Now a howling squalling infant,
Dragging at its mother's skirt,
Seems annoyed and rather peevish,
As it bellows in the dirt.
When the mother, losing patience,
Slaps it hard — a real good go,
That's one of many incidents,
That make the passing show.

Round the indicator gathered,
Is a group of shearers too,
You can tell them by their baggage,
Going south a 'shed' to do.
They laugh and joke and scramble,
One is drunk and singing low,
But they look content and happy,
As they watched the passing show.

There's a magsman* flash and cheeky,
Looking out for likely mugs,
Sights a 'D'† who knows his history,
And the post more closely hugs.
For you'll always seem him waiting,
Whenever you may go,
Up around the Central station,
To survey the passing show.

*   *   *

Steaming to a picnic

Picnic trains were part of rail's heyday — and no more so than
in Maryborough, Queensland. In the early 1960s, there were not
enough carriages based there to cope with the picnic train outings,
so suburban carriages would be hauled up from Brisbane over
preceding days. These trains were a rail enthusiast's dream: often
they would be pulled by two PB15 4-6-0 locomotives with an
astonishing assortment of carriages behind them, some having

---

* Confidence trickster
† Detective

been in service since the 1880s, and including old parlour cars, drawing room and sleeping cars that had been converted for suburban passenger duties.

In 1963, on picnic day, six trains would set out and travel down the Pialba branch to the seaside location of Urangan. On 31 October 1963, it required a great deal of planning and organisation at Urangan which had a comparatively small yard. That day picnic trains arrived at 9.09 am, 9.29 am, 10.14 am, 10.41 am, 11.32 am and 11.55 am. At the end of the day the no doubt weary and sunburnt picnickers were loaded on to trains leaving at 4.30 pm, 5.00 pm, 5.20 pm, 6.00 pm, 6.30 pm and 6.55 pm. It was a long day, the rail workers and their families from Kingaroy the last to get home — at 1.11 am the next morning.

In a 1965 picnic outing, one observer of the Urangan yard counted six PB15 locomotives, thirty-eight carriages and a two-car 2000 railmotors all crammed into the yard. The last picnic trains to Urangan ran in 1972.

*   *   *

Laverton — eventually

Passenger services, in the pre-motor car era, existed almost everywhere the rails went. A narrow gauge line was laid northwards from the West Australian gold mining town of Kalgoorlie to service other new mining centres, the first section being opened in 1899 with the rails reaching Leonora in 1903. This, along with a spur from the midway station of Malcolm to Laverton which opened two years later, for some time sustained a daily passenger train over its 259 km length to service the mining communities dotted along its path. Many now long-forgotten stations — Paddington, Broad Arrow, Scotia, Comet Value, Yunndaga, Jessop's Well and Gwalia — burst into life as the lifeline from the south arrived.

However, by 1953 if you wanted to travel from Kalgoorlie up the narrow gauge line to Laverton, you needed patience. Your choices were Train 197 on Thursdays which was a diesel-electric railcar or, on either Tuesdays or Fridays, locomotive-hauled

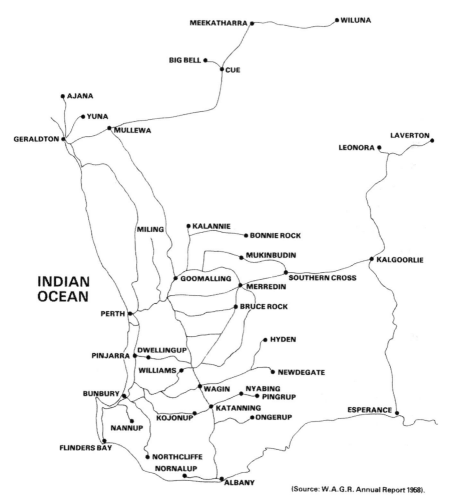

(Source: W.A.G.R. Annual Report 1958).

The split line to Leonora and Laverton is clearly illustrated on this map of the Western Australia railway system as it was in 1958 and before the era of closures got under way. It also shows the density of lines in the main wheat-growing areas.

Train 191 which was designated as 'fast goods, car attached'. There was a catch: both 197 and 191 had two destinations because once those trains reached the junction stop of Malcolm the line divided, one section running to Leonora, the other to Laverton.

With the railcar, the service left Kalgoorlie at 10.30 am and reached Malcolm at 4.21 pm. If you wanted to go to Leonora, all was fine and good — the railcar pulled out of Malcolm after a three minute stop and you reached your destination at 5.00 pm. But what if you wanted to go on the Laverton section, to Laverton itself or the intermediate stations of Murrin Murrin or Morgans? In your case, you cooled your heels at Malcolm for 1 hr 29 mins at the end of which time the railcar arrived back from Leonora. Then you got on board for the journey on the other section of the divided line to Laverton, which was reached at 8.10 pm.

It could have been worse. And it certainly was if you chose the 'fast goods, car attached'. It drifted into Malcolm at 7.35 pm and Laverton passengers waited there until 2.10 am the next morning at which time the 'fast goods' pulled out of Malcolm and deposited its passengers on the platform at Laverton at 6.00 am, eighteen hours and ten minutes after departing from Kalgoorlie.

2

First Railways

A TRAMWAY USING IRON rails was laid in Newcastle (New South Wales) in 1827 for use by the Australian Agricultural Company. But, while this was the first recorded use of rail transport in Australia, it fails to qualify as a 'railway' in our history context in that it did not act as a common carrier, nor did it operate scheduled services. The same has to be said for the convict tramway opened in 1836 at Port Arthur, Tasmania. There was also a horse-drawn tramway which began operating in 1854 at the mouth of the Murray River in South Australia, between Goolwa and Port Elliot, a distance of eleven kilometres. All worthy of note, but not railways for the purpose of this book. What follows is the record of the first railways in each colony (later state) and territory.

Victoria pioneers steam rail

That first steam-hauled ran between Melbourne and Sandridge (later Port Melbourne) on 12 September 1854. That first train pulled out of Flinders Street station at 12.20 pm; it consisted of a third class open car carrying the band of the 40th Regiment, a first class car for the Lieutenant-Governor, Sir Charles Hotham, and the directors of the Melbourne and Hobsons Bay Railway Company, along with two second class carriages for other guests. This line now serves as a light rail route.

New South Wales

A year later, on 26 September 1855, the Sydney-Parramatta line was opened. The Sydney Railway Company had begun, on 10 October 1849, to lay a line from the colony's capital with the intention of going as far as Goulburn but was unable to continue as a viable business. In 1855 the company was acquired by the New South Wales government which completed the line as far as Parramatta, a distance of 22 km.

An early scene in New South Wales. It is Goulburn in 1879 with a freight train having just arrived from Sydney behind 0-6-0 No. 21 with a rake of open D wagons and a brake van. State Records NSW.

South Australia

On 21 April 1856 a broad gauge line was opened between Adelaide and Port Adelaide by that colony's government. Construction had begun in 1853. The government had taken over from the original promoters the responsibility for the construction of the line.

Queensland

The first line (between Ipswich and Bigge's Camp, now Grandchester) was opened on 31 July 1865. In the early years of the new colony, goods moving between Brisbane and Ipswich had gone by river, and the remainder of the transport link from Ipswich had been served by horse-drawn coaches and bullock teams hauling wagons. The privately owned Moreton Bay Tramway Company had drawn up plans for a horse-drawn tramway between Ipswich and Toowoomba but could not raise sufficient capital. The new colony's government interceded and opted to construct a mechanically powered railway.

Tasmania

Private enterprise in the form of the Launceston and Western Railway Company built the island state's first line, the 72 km route between Launceston and Deloraine. It was laid to the broad gauge of 5ft 3in (1,600 mm) and opened on 10 February 1871. A banquet of forty dishes was held at Launceston's town hall to celebrate the event.

Western Australia

The first government-owned line was opened in 1879 between Geraldton and Northampton, a distance of 53 km. It was built to serve lead and copper mines inland from the port of Geraldton. The government's first plan had been to lay the track to a three-foot

(914 mm) gauge to save money. But privately-owned timber company lines already in operation had been laid to 3ft 6in (1,067 mm) and the government decided to go with that gauge, a change that added £18,000 to the cost of construction.

Northern Territory

A rail line between Darwin and Pine Creek opened on 1 October 1889. This was the planned first stage of the North Australia Railway which would eventually reach and peter out at a desolate spot called Birdum, and which was to have formed part of the north-south transcontinental railway. The NAR closed in 1976, the Commonwealth Railways no longer being able to justify the losses combined with the deterioration of the line.

Australian Capital Territory

A line of 10 km in length was built from Queanbeyan just across the border with New South Wales to link with the Goulburn-Bombala line, so allowing NSW trains to run into Canberra. The first train ran on the line on 25 May 1914. Passenger services began on the line from 15 October 1923. There were also plans (never implemented) drawn up to build a line from Canberra to the other slice of the Australian Capital Territory, the reserve at Jervis Bay on the Tasman Sea coastline. This area had also been carved out of NSW so that the ACT could have its own port.

3

Life in the Railway Age

OF ALL THE TORMENTS suffered by the railway traveller in Australia — and there were many — none was so great as the break of gauge. At state borders, and within states (at places such as Kalgoorlie in Western Australia or Terowie in South Australia), it was often impossible to complete a rail journey without passing through one of the many stations at which the track width changed from one gauge to another, the legacy of Australian colonies building their railways to their own needs without account for what was happening elsewhere. Western Australia and Queensland had gone for the narrow gauge of 3ft 6in (1,067 mm). New South Wales opted for standard gauge of 4ft 8½ inches (1,435 mm) while Victoria went for the broad, or Irish, gauge of 5ft 3in (1,600 mm). South Australia went one better by having two gauges (narrow and broad) and then a third (standard) once the Commonwealth Railways started building the transcontinental line, leading to the phenomenon of triple-gauge stations where all three systems met.

Tasmania opted for narrow gauge but, being an island, that never caused any part of the gauge nightmare.

But, on the mainland, nightmare it was when a train reached the extremity of its system and the rest of the journey had to be completed on another gauge. There was usually a rush from one train to the other as passengers vied to get the best seats on the waiting carriages. It was not unknown for the second train to have fewer cars than the first one, so that some passengers would be left without seats. Tempers would be short as people would wrestle their luggage from one train to the other. It was worse at night as a change of gauge meant that passengers in sleeping cars had to get up, dress and cart their luggage across the platform in the early hours of the morning. Even Melbourne travellers who wanted sleeping compartments on the journey to Sydney found they had to sit up until 10.00 pm, at which time Victoria's plush (but without sleeping compartments) broad gauge Spirit of Progress reached Albury. Only then could they transfer to New South Wales standard gauge rolling stock and settle down in bunks for a night's sleep. Coming the other way, the traveller would be woken up in the early hours of the morning once the train from Sydney had slid into Albury's long platform in order to make the transfer to the waiting, sitting cars-only Victorian train. Luggage would have to be closed up, the children gathered out of their beds and a porter hailed to make the transfer.

The American writer Mark Twain, recording in 1897 his travels in Australia, told readers what the interchange at Albury involved.

At the frontier between New South Wales and Victoria our multitude of passengers were routed out of their snug beds by lantern-light in the morning in the biting cold of a high altitude to change cars on a road that has no break in it from Sydney to Melbourne! Think of the paralysis of intellect that gave that idea birth; imagine the boulder it emerged from on some petrified legislator's shoulders. It is a narrow-gauge road to the frontier, and a broader gauge thence to Melbourne. The two governments were the builders of the road and are the owners of it. One or two reasons are given for this curious state of things. One is, that it represents the jealousy existing between the colonies — the two most important colonies of Australasia. What the other one is, I have forgotten. But it is of no consequence. It could be but another effort to explain the inexplicable. All passengers fret at the double-gauge; all shippers of freight must of course fret at it; unnecessary expense, delay, and annoyance are imposed upon everybody concerned, and no one is benefited.

He also had plenty to say about the standard of the rolling stock. His conclusion was that the Australian colonies had spent so much on grandiose railway stations (such as the one at Maryborough, Victoria) that they had to economise on the trains themselves:

> Why, that train from Maryborough will consist of eighteen freight-cars [wagons] and two passenger kennels; cheap, poor, shabby, slovenly; no drinking water, no sanitation arrangements, every imaginable inconvenience; and slow? — oh, the gait of slow molasses; no air-brake, no springs, and they'll jolt your head off every time they start or stop ... They spend tons of money to house you palatially while you wait fifteen minutes for a train, then degrade you to six hours' convict transportation to get the foolish outlay back.

In winter, the cold weather in the dead of the night was another thing to be borne with fortitude by rail travellers as they moved between trains. At 5.00 am in South Australia on the Broken Hill Express heading for Adelaide there came the dreaded call: 'Terowie — change trains'. Thereupon passengers coming from Broken Hill in New South Wales who had travelled through the night on the narrow gauge train, reached Terowie, at which point the line became broad gauge, and went out into the bitter cold of the morning to their next train.

Endurance was a quality much needed in the rail traveller. Take the trip to Brisbane from Sydney by rail before 1 May 1889 (after which date the Hawkesbury River was bridged). The train pulled out of Sydney at 4.53 pm, terminating at River Wharf, Brooklyn, at 6.30 pm. The railways department then allowed one hour and fifteen minutes for the transfer across the Hawkesbury River with the steamer *General Gordon* carrying all the passengers, luggage and mail to Mullet Creek for loading on to another train. There the Northern Mail awaited, ready for a 7.45 pm departure. Next morning, passengers in the sleeping compartments were woken early and told their cars would be coming off when the train arrived at West Tamworth (still in New South Wales) by 7.00 am, with the annoyed travellers having to get out of bed, pack and move to sitting cars.

The train reached the border town of Wallangarra, where the New South Wales standard gauge met the Queensland narrow gauge, at 5.00 pm the following day. A connecting Queensland Government Railways narrow gauge train pulled out thirty minutes later, reaching Brisbane at 6.05 am on the third day of the journey.

Hayden Biggs, recording in 1938 his memories of early rail travel for the railway news sheet *Bulletin*, remembered deciding to go to the Royal National Park near Sydney, the branch line having opened in March 1886. He arrived at Redfern station to find that the 10.25 am train had already departed for the then newest extension to Sydney's suburban rail network. Then a rake of cattle wagons was backed into one of the Redfern platforms and the waiting passengers told to board for the Royal National Park. They proceeded to their destination at an average 16 km/h, no doubt in discomfort.

Fifteen years later, Glaswegian geologist J. W. Gregory and his university party set out on 31 December 1901 from Adelaide to Hergott Springs (later Marree), on what was then South Australia's Great Northern Railway to Oodnadatta. He recounted that the rails had been laid with the great daily variations of temperature in mind (contracting at night, expanding during the heat of the day) and the resultant gaps between lengths of rail meant speed restrictions for trains. Moreover, missing a train meant considerable delays: between Quorn and Hergott Springs the service operated every other day; Hergott Springs to Coward Springs once a week; and beyond to Oodnadatta only once a fortnight. Gregory reported that almost everything required to maintain the barren south-west of Queensland — from customs books to police officers — had to come from Brisbane, the state capital. But there was no railway from Brisbane to the most western part of Queensland where it bordered South Australia, so all parts of the state government service had to go south through New South Wales, then through Victoria to Melbourne, then across western Victoria into South Australia and then, finally, back up the Great Northern Railway, for a final horse-drawn road connection back into Queensland. In all, it was a journey of 4,105 km.

As that Queensland example shows, while some of the train journeys in early Australia were certainly arduous, the alternative was normally worse. Before Melbourne and Adelaide were fully linked by train services a journey from the Victorian capital to the South Australian capital involved boarding a train that left Melbourne for Casterton, that which took more than twelve hours overnight with no sleeping cars. Then there was a twenty-four hour journey by horse-drawn road coach to Naracoorte in South Australia, then on to another train as far as Kingston. Thence it was a road coach again, followed by a four-hour journey by steamer across Lakes Albert and Alexandrina to Port Milang, with the exhausted passengers ending at their destination four days after setting out.

But even as recently as fifty years ago, rail could still be a slow way to get anywhere. Take the obscure Kunama branch in New South Wales which ran off another branch, the Cootamundra to Tumut line. The Kunama line, 34.7 km in total, was a late addition to the system, having been opened on 17 December 1923 to handle fruit traffic from around Batlow as well as timber. By 1954, the line was served by a mixed train (that is, goods wagons with a passenger car attached), usually pulled by a 19 class 0-6-0 locomotive. The line boasted the longest stretch of 1-in-25 gradient in the state; the track climbed 455 metres in 16 km and the steepness meant a train could start out on the flat section with a load of 250 tons, but was allowed only 100 tons beyond Wereboldera station. The speed limit for the branch was 40 km/h, but on the steep climb up the side of the valley towards Batlow the train was down to less than 13 km/h which, as one writer put it, 'gives ample opportunity to view the scenery'. Moreover, drivers were required to stop the train at three specified points along the branch and check the hand brakes.

Even on main lines, speed was not always the thing. The 228 km journey in the 1950s from Port Pirie to Adelaide took four and a half hours, resulting from twenty-three intermediate stops and, usually, a heavy load of up to fifteen carriages and five wagons containing fresh produce for the Adelaide market that proved a heavy, slow haul for the steam locomotive at the head.

The comforts of train travel varied. By 1897, the intercolonial trains between Adelaide and Melbourne were equipped with McLaren's patented foot-warmers. These contained acetate of soda and could be heated by immersion for fifteen minutes in a tank of boiling water, retaining heat for up to eight hours. They could, after that, be shaken and would warm up again for a period. Queensland Government Railways introduced foot-warmers in 1911 on the overnight train from Brisbane to the border crossing at Wallangarra, then eventually in other mail trains in the winter months. They were allocated on the basis of one for every three first-class passengers and stayed in use until 1958.

Eventually some of the railway systems adopted heating of carriages by running steam from the locomotives through pipes into the passenger cars. By 1952, the New South Wales Government Railways had adapted fifty carriages for steam heating and twenty-eight locomotives were equipped to pump the steam to the cars behind. The steam from the locomotive's boiler passed through a reducing valve which lowered its pressure and then it was pumped to pipes contained within cylinders on the carriage floors. Between 1 May and 30 September each year, the cars were heated in this manner, the passengers being able to adjust the heat in their own section of the car. The Federal City Express to Canberra and the Southern Highlands Express to Goulburn, along with some of the overnight mail trains running to western destinations, were among those provided with this new heating system.

Ron Fitch, who spent much of his railway career in Western Australia before rising to Commissioner at South Australian

Railways, recalled that the mixed trains in the western state ambled along at an average 27 km/h. The passengers were subjected to the risk of whiplash due to the loose couplings on goods wagons assembled between the locomotive and the passenger cars. If there were livestock vans in the consist, the smell from the animals and their droppings were clearly discernible in the carriages.

'Express' was a term used rather loosely. For example, the Kalgoorlie Express stopped at thirty-five stations between Northam and Kalgoorlie with an average speed of 37 km/h, while the Broken Hill Express ground to a halt at twenty-nine stopping places between Gawler and Broken Hill. Passengers in the sitting cars of the Kalgoorlie train, should they have needed a drink of water, had to walk out on to the open end platform of the car where there was a canvas water bag from which hung a small drinking vessel. This was a common practice in various parts of the Australian rail network.

For those who travelled by train in the heyday of rail, there was nothing quite like it; it was an atmosphere that died with the move to buses, aeroplanes and the private car. Lloyd Holmes, a railwayman and later author, wrote in 1965 of his childhood memories of being at Sydney Steam Station, recalling the:

> ... rush and bustle, the smell of newsprint and fruit, people streaming in all directions, luggage trolleys and loudspeakers adding to the din and the sheer youthful wonder of standing beside a hot, steaming 38 Class, just arrived from Albury, a dead pigeon lying below the smokebox as mute testimony to its speed.

A busy day in Binnaway

Trains brought life — often only for the duration of the train's stay — to many towns around Australia. An account by L.A. Clark in the rail magazine *Bulletin* of a journey between Dubbo and Werris Creek in New South Wales illustrated how the small town of Binnaway, located 453 km from Sydney by rail and with a population then of fewer than eight hundred people, became a place of noise and bustle three days a week. The town was on the route of trains travelling east to west, others coming up the Wallerawang to Merrygoen line (via Mudgee) and it was the junction for the 145 km branch northwards to Coonabarabran and Gwabegar.

All passengers travelling between on the main regional line between Dubbo and Werris Creek had to change trains at Binnaway because the lines from the respective towns came together outside Binnaway and then ran into the station in parallel. The station had a refreshment room, ample sidings (which were needed, as we will see), a turntable and locomotive roundhouse. Passenger trains were at this time normally hauled by either 12 class or 30T class locomotives. On one of the three days when the station was at its busiest, the action would begin at 10.54 am when the train arrived from Werris Creek; passengers disembarked, the van was unloaded at the platform and the van and carriages were then shunted into one of the sidings while the locomotive went to be serviced for its next trip.

At 12.18 pm the train from Sydney via Mudgee arrived; its passengers disembarked, that van was unloaded and then the carriages were shunted off to another siding. By this time, the platform was covered with luggage as the passengers waited for connections to their various onward destinations. At 12.42 pm, the diesel railmotor pulled in from Dubbo; more luggage was deposited on the platform.

Finally, at 1.06 pm, a second diesel train arrived, this time from Gwabegar. It came in on the loop to pass the diesel set already sitting at the platform, then reversed back into the platform so it now had a clear run for its onward trip. Even more luggage was unloaded. This meant that, apart from any travellers whose destination was Binnaway itself, four train-loads of passengers were milling about, some having been there for more than two hours. To add to the activity on the sidings as carriages were stored temporarily, a goods train usually turned up during this three-hour rush period. Eventually, the dispersal began (at 1.25 pm) when one diesel train departed for Dubbo, and then five minutes later the other accelerated away from the platform bound for Gwabegar. Following their departure, one of the locomotive-hauled train consists — having been reassembled — reversed into the platform, loaded its passengers and departed for Werris Creek at 1.55 pm.

At 2.05 pm, the last of the train departures took place as the steam engine and its carriages slid out of the platform bound for Sydney via Merrygoen and Mudgee. Then silence returned to Binnaway station.

All the way by rail

Just after the Second World War, it was possible for a traveller in Australia to make a continuous rail journey of more than 7,400 km from Wiluna in the Western Australian goldfields to Mount Isa in Queensland. It required nine changes of train along the way, first at Mullewa, then Perth, as passengers transferred to other West Australian trains. At Kalgoorlie there was another change, this time because the West Australian narrow gauge met the standard gauge of the transcontinental line. At Port Augusta, that standard gauge line met the South Australian narrow gauge system, so trains had to be changed again and then again at Broken Hill, where the narrow gauge of South Australia met the New South Wales standard gauge.

At Sydney, it was a matter of transferring from the Western line express to the train travelling north to the Queensland border where, at Wallangarra, the standard gauge met Queensland's narrow gauge. Our (by now) very weary traveller could rest for a few hours as the train trundled across Queensland until Brisbane was reached where he or she had to transfer to yet another train, this one running north to Townsville; at that station, it was time to transfer to the last train for the final leg inland to Mount Isa.

Each of the various state railway departments employed vast numbers of staff at the hundreds of manned stations spread around the country. But it was the termini in the various state capitals that were the epicentre of railway bustle, and some remain so today in spite of decades of depredation of long-distance railway services. Holiday times were always busy at the big city stations; these usually began with the departure of all the boarding school pupils for their homes. The stalls in the main concourses would have been well stocked with pies and comics; but good behaviour on the train would have been maintained. In New South Wales, it was common practice to have the schoolchildren in their own carriage so that the guard could keep a close eye on what went on there. And, for those travelling in Queensland who wanted to freshen up after a long and sooty trip, it was possible to have a bath at Brisbane, Rockhampton or Townsville stations; at Mackay and Cairns, shower rooms were available.

Victoria's Railway Commissioner, Harold Clapp, did much to help bewildered long-distance passengers by introducing the 'Man in Grey' — a person who stood on the main concourse and whose job was to answer all the questions posed by people trying to find the right platform and train. Between 1933 and 1942, Spencer Street station in Melbourne boasted a room where mothers could change their babies and heat baby food.

In 1916, South Australian Railways (SAR) decided that passengers suffering from either cancer or tuberculosis could ask a stationmaster to reserve a compartment for them although, in the same year, SAR employees were told not to provide physical assistance to those with infectious diseases. By 1922, licensed luggage porters were provided at Adelaide station and ordinary uniformed porters were no longer required to help passengers with their luggage. Two years later, SAR began providing luggage delivery to the better inner city hotels and clubs.

4

Snapshots of Railway Life

Goods of all descriptions

Trains once carried just about everything. If you lived in the country before reliable road transport and you wanted a piano, the only way to have it sent was by train to your nearest station. Trains also once carried live rabbits, rabbit meat, tallow and fat, along with all the main food staples in the form of grains, fruit and vegetables. Queensland's railways saw seasonal work from the pineapple crop, the Dorrigo branch in northern New South Wales hauled away the district's annual potato harvest; in the southern part of that state, the Crookwell branch carried the output of a small iron ore mine.

Circuses were once big customers for the railways. In 1963, the Wirth's Circus Train travelling to Mildura, Victoria, was made up of forty-eight vehicles, including seven carriages for the staff and performers and nine wagons with especially raised roofs to contain the larger animals.

And then there was the mail. The first Travelling Post Office was introduced in 1887, on the Queensland network, and by 1911 these vehicles were attached to many long-distance trains. At the small rail siding of Lurnea, a local landowner would use a red flag to signal for the mail train to stop so that he could post letters and parcels with the TPO van.

If you lived at Harden, on the Main South line in New South Wales, and belonged to a wine society that delivered by the case (even as late as 1960), that wine came by rail and you went down to the station to collect it.

In 1867, Queensland's rail system issued parcel stamps, the same size as the postal variety and also bearing Queen Victoria's head. Later, the parcel stamps became much larger in size and bore the name of the station from which the parcel was consigned. Eventually, Queensland Government Railways offered delivery to your door service in Brisbane, Toowoomba, Bundaberg, Mount Morgan, Townsville and Mackay. In 1958, for example, QGR had thirteen lorries in Brisbane just delivering parcels to businesses and homes.

Of great benefit to people in country Queensland was the system of cash-on-delivery which operated from 1905 until 1980, the payment covering both the purchase from the store and delivery.

Taking Care

The railways tended to take care of their own. When, in the early 1950s, Reg Latemore, the ganger at Womallila (a station on Queensland's Western line) died of heart failure, his widow was given a job as stationmistress at Blaxland near Dalby so that she could support their four children.

In the nineteenth century, a Mrs Delaney, the widow of a man killed by a Tasmanian Government Railways train, was granted a free lifetime pass to travel between Rhyndaston and Parattah; she became a familiar figure selling apples on the expresses which ran between Hobart and Launceston. Mrs Delaney was known for her ready wit and her sharp replies.

Not always cheap at the price

The advance of the railway into Australia's regions was aimed at providing cheap, safe and fast transport for country people and their produce. But it also brought benefits to those regions by making possible visits to regional centres by all types of entertainers. Once the rail reached Albury on the New South Wales-Victoria border, for example, Sydney musicians began visiting the town to give philharmonic concerts. However, rail was still not all that cheap a mode of transport in its earliest days. When the first revenue train departed from Ballarat for Melbourne on 10 April 1862 it carried only four passengers — not surprising considering that the fare was 26 shillings, almost half the then average weekly wage of three pounds.

What every good driver and fireman needed

Nothing was easy work in the early decades of the railways. In the era before cranes, it was a daily task to carry coal by hand to the locomotives.

Steam locomotives in New South Wales in the nineteenth century were typically equipped with the following:

- One shovel
- Two tins of oil for lubricating side rods, wheel boxes, pistons and air pumps.
- A hand lamp with white, green and red shades if signalling was required.

- A bucket.
- Two cans for dispensing oil.
- Two flare lamps.
- One brush.
- A bottle of kerosene.
- Cotton waste.
- Spanners.
- Syringe to remove water from wheel boxes.
- A pack of detonators to place on the track (in times of emergency) to warn other trains.

Nothing was easy work in the early decades of the railways, the days before cranes; this meant hard toil to fill the locomotive tender with coal. These railwaymen at Petersburg (later Peterborough), South Australia, are fuelling a Y-class locomotive by use of wicker baskets. The photo dates from the 1890s. John Mannion Collection.

After the rails are gone

There are mining ghost towns, and railway ones. Morgan in South Australia was once the second biggest South Australian port after Adelaide thanks to the railway and its location on the 'Grand Bend' on the Murray River. It became an important transhipment point. The Kapunda railway was extended to reach the river at Morgan (South Australian Railways named the station North West Bend) and it was opened for traffic on 18 October 1878. The line ran to the then newly built wharf, sixty-metres long and nine metres above the river level, at which paddle steamers and trains exchanged cargoes. At the zenith of its importance, Morgan saw six trains a day leaving for Adelaide on the broad gauge line. But inevitably the river traffic was lost to rail and road. Morgan lost its railway branch line on 2 November 1969.

How to lose money

While country people inevitably fought the closure of their railway lines, many of these branches were a burden on the taxpayer for much if not all of their lives. The Tumbarumba branch in southern New South Wales was such a case. This 130 km line from Wagga Wagga was a loss-maker from the start. The first section, to Humula, cost £355,152 to build (and was opened in 1917). In its first full year of operation, the line earned £5,754 with the cost of operating the section amounting to £8,143. This was not much of a return on the capital investment in an era where there was no real competition from road transport. The final section to Tumbarumba was opened in 1921, having added an additional £412,405 to the overall construction cost. Nature came to the taxpayers' rescue in 1974, with a flood washing away part of the line and ensuring its permanent closure.

The most under-used railway

In 1927 the Victorian government authorised the building of a line from Robinvale on the Murray River, over that waterway and over the state border into New South Wales and then on another 48.5 km to a point the map marked Lette. The ground along the proposed line was not inviting, being mainly sandy scrub land capable of supporting the occasional wheat crop but only with the most propitious weather conditions. A road–rail bridge was built across the Murray complete with a central lifting span. Laying of rail continued until, when a distance of 22.5 km from Robinvale had been reached, work was suspended. By this time it was 1929 and the economic conditions were such that there was a contraction in government spending. But three stations, complete with platforms and sidings, had been provided at Euston, Benanee and Koorake. The Railway Construction Branch retained control and ran the line on a 'trains as required' basis. Between 1929 and 1935 the average use of the line was one train a year. The line was abandoned in 1935.

Loco in Hobart

At its main Hobart station Tasmanian Government Railways had, for many years, primitive safe working arrangements. There was no signalling or interlocking until 1922; only then was a signal box installed at Hobart Junction at the outer end of the yards. Before that, locomotives operated within the Hobart yard on a staff and ticket system, a system normally applied only on sections of open line (to ensure that no more than one train was on that section at any given time).

Mine, and mine alone

If you were important enough, in an earlier age you could have your own railway platform. Several influential people who lived

CHAPTER 4: SNAPSHOTS OF RAILWAY LIFE

in the Blue Mountains (to the west of Sydney) were recipients of this special treatment. Near Lapstone, John Lucas, a member of the Legislative Assembly (the lower house in the New South Wales parliament), could walk down to Lucasville, his own concrete platform on the rail line to Sydney. Eager's Platform was provided on the same line for Sir Geoffrey Eager (it later became a public station called The Valley, now Valley Heights). Numantia was a platform for the personal use of Sir James Martin; it had been a public station until 1891, but from then until closure in 1897 it was reserved to be used only by the Martin family and the neighbouring Cliff family. There was a platform near the Lapstone Hotel called Breakfast Point which until 1892 was for the exclusive use of a Mr Want.

For prisoners and greyhounds

A survey of New South Wales rolling stock rosters between 1892 and 1938 showed the government system had available at various times seven four-wheeled wagons and four eight-wheeled wagons which were used as prison vans. From 1890 the rail fleet included a four-wheeled invalid car. The fleet also had more than 170 four-wheeled and twelve eight-wheeled horse boxes, not to mention the four pigeon vans. In 1935 the railway department got an addition by way of DC 1040, a twelve-wheeled dental car (that year joining FW 76, a hospital car, and four RG class eight-wheeled greyhound wagons on the state's rolling stock roster).

A state of jealousy

In 1889, Victorian Railways published a new by-law which allowed a rebate on goods transported to and from Melbourne by train into and from the Riverina region of New South Wales. The purpose was transparent: to induce farmers in the colony to Victoria's north to send their produce to Melbourne rather than Sydney and also to buy their supplies from Victoria. At this stage, the only broad gauge line into NSW was the line from the Victorian border to Deniliquin owned by the Deniliquin and Moama Railway Company. In the 1920s, it would be joined by the extensions of three other Victorian lines into NSW — the 192.4 km of track in NSW to Balranald, the new 62.1 km to Stony Crossing and 61.5 km laid to Oaklands. There was also a short section across the Murray to link up with the NSW standard gauge railhead at Tocumwal. The rebate meant that a Riverina farmer could pay freight charges of 67 shillings and threepence for a ton of fencing wire carted from Melbourne, against the 80 shillings he would pay having its railed from Sydney. Grocery consignments attracted a freight charge of 72 shillings and sixpence from Melbourne, rather than the 86 shillings and eight pence it would cost getting them from Sydney.

The shortest-lived government line

On 24 August 1922 Western Australian Government Railways purchased the 26.6 km line built just eighteen months earlier by the Swan Portland Cement Company, running from Waroona to Lake Clifton, and which branched off the Perth-Bunbury corridor. The cement company needed the line to transport lime from Lake Clifton. Soon after the government took over the track, however, the lime works closed and thereafter the railway had little purpose. The track was closed on 31 December 1924 (with rails and sleepers used on building the Lake Grace-Newdegate wheat line completed in 1926).

Special occasions

Starting of work on, or opening of, a railway line was an occasion for celebration. Such an occasion signified the political importance of the railways, and leading colonial dignitaries were keen to be associated with them. But new lines also excited the population; their lives had hitherto contained few distractions from the daily grind; the railway, however, signalled the transformation of those lives. They could henceforth travel to towns more quickly and, now, goods and produce they ordered from those same towns arrived far more promptly than when the came by cart, a process that would have taken weeks in some cases.

The turning of the first sod, or the arrival of the first train, brought out all the locals in their best clothes. Huge banquets would ensue. The laying of the foundation stone for Geelong's railway station was a mere preliminary to the feasting that was to follow: the directors of the Geelong and Melbourne Railway Company catered not only for the invited guests but also for those who just turned up to watch. In the case of the latter, there was provided a roasted bullock and barrels of beer. The company spent £1,000 on the day, a fabulous sum at the time.

Seven thousand people turned up to cheer when the railway reached the Victorian town of Castlemaine in 1862. Victoria's governor, Sir Henry Barkly, was on hand for the occasion. There was a sit-down banquet for three hundred people, the tables covered with huge pyramids of fruit. The day ended with a grand ball.

Livestock

Cattle, sheep and pig cartage was an important part of the railway business in most parts of Australia, none more so than in Queensland. Dajarra in the far north was reputed to be the busiest cattle transfer station in the world; Cunnamulla and Quilpie were among other stations that saw huge livestock consignments as cattle and mobs of sheep passed through the rail yards.

Queensland Railways installed water sprays at Charleville and Flaggy Rock to help cool cattle being transported and by 1926 it was the rule that pigs had to be sprayed in transit to stop them getting too hot. Cattle on long hauls had to be unloaded after twenty-four hours to allow them to take water and walk about (these long duration hauls mostly disappeared after diesel haulage became common, although livestock trains were always given high priority for clearance, second only to mail trains). Those shipping cattle received a free ticket for their drovers, one ticket for each three bogie wagons paid for.

At Jericho, Monty Head, who worked for Queensland Railways, remembers that even in the 1960s there were three or four men employed to feed and water the livestock while the animals were in the yard pens. As many as thirty K wagons would be loaded for each livestock train. A count in 1926 put the Jericho shire's sheep population at 1.25 million (the town was also a head-quarters for shearing gangs). Even in the 1950s, and in the last years of steam, twenty-seven train crews lived in Jericho, along with fifteen fettlers, the stationmaster and two assistant stationmasters. On average, eleven trains a day passed through Jericho. Another important business for this and many other stations was wool, with bales hand loaded on to wagons.

Rails in the road

A railway line running down a busy street was very much a South Australia thing. The Adelaide-Glenelg line had sections at each end on roadways (King William Street in the centre of Adelaide and Jetty Road at the other), while the branch from Adelaide to Semaphore had its terminus at the latter located on a busy street. At Port Adelaide there were railway lines running along both St Vincent and Lipson streets.

But Port Pirie took the cake. In 1875 the narrow gauge line to the port town from Peterborough was laid down Ellen Street, the main thoroughfare. By 1889, and with the growth of the lead smelting operations, it was felt that Ellen Street should have a station befitting Port Pirie's importance. There was constructed an ornate building (along the lines of the Brighton Pavilion in England) with a clock-less tower and a ticket box opening on to the footpath. There was no raised platform; passengers simply walked out into the street and climbed up into carriages. Trains were limited to four miles an hour in Ellen Street and passenger trains could have as many as fifteen carriages; these passenger trains could also have attached wagons to be loaded with market garden produce destined for Adelaide, with lorries arriving with peas,

A picnic trains for workers at the nearby lead smelter inches its way along Ellen Street in Port Pirie in 1964. John Mannion Collection.

tomatoes and various fresh vegetables and the loads being transferred to the wagons in the middle of the street. It was not until
1967 that road traffic won, and the Port Pirie station was moved
away from the main street.

Towns the railways made

Australia's railways made or dominated many towns throughout Australia. Most of these were in regional areas. Most had as
their main imperative operational needs. In New South Wales,
Murrurundi and Valley Heights stabled banking locomotives that,
in the days of steam, would be added to trains to assist on steep
grades in the area; Alpha in Queensland also provided the same
service to help battle the steep climb out of Bogantungan, the
locomotive depot being — unusually — at the top of the grade
but that is where good supplies of water were found. This meant
that, every time they were needed for the 12.9 km grind up the
hill, the steam engines would first run light over the 72 km from
Alpha to Bogantungan to pick up their trains.

Where they were large rail depots, with the necessary drivers,
firemen and guards, so also there had to be administrators (sometimes as high in rank as district traffic managers), gangs of fettlers,
cleaners, shunters and shed hands. In some of these railway towns,
as many as sixty per cent of the workers would be employed by
the railway.

Breaks of gauge were another reason for large railway com-
plements, such as in Albury, New South Wales, and Terowie in
South Australia; the latter was during the Second World War
a major military transfer point and the place at which General
Douglas MacArthur made his famous pledge of 'I shall return' to
the Philippines.

Junee in New South Wales grew out of nothing. In 1947 it had the state's largest locomotive roundhouse, engines that were needed to work the main line between Sydney and Melbourne and the vast network of branch lines through the Riverina region. Further north, Werris Creek served not only the main lines passing through, but the various lines radiating out over northern NSW; before dieselisation occurred, the station was the base for eight hundred railway employees.

In South Australia, there was Peterborough and its three gauges. It had the biggest workshops in the state outside Adelaide; at its zenith, the Peterborough sub-division employed about 1,800 people. The district superintendent's house had an attached schoolroom used to instruct staff in railway rules.

5

Refreshing the Traveller

WHILE MUCH OF RAIL travel meant enduring the rudimentary, there were flashes of style and comfort. Douglas MacGregor remembers travelling from his home at Cunnamulla, Queensland, to Brisbane in the late 1940s. The consist of wooden carriages on the old train offered the traveller a choice between first and second class sleepers, and a dining car was attached to the train as far as Mitchell, where it was stabled until being attached to the returning service from Brisbane. After this dining car was taken off at Mitchell, there were plenty of opportunities for passengers to buy food and drinks when the train stopped at subsequent stations down the line: Miles, Chinchilla, Dalby, Toowoomba and Helidon all had refreshment rooms. While the dining car was attached, passengers could sit down to three-course meals, complete with silver service, and could also take morning and afternoon tea in the car. The task for the staff aboard the dining car was not easy; there was no refrigeration, so ice blocks were taken aboard to help keep the food fresh in the searing summer heat. The cook, apart

from the need constantly to stoke the wood stove, had to contend
with an often uneven track. To make sure the soup would not
spill, it had to be heated in a large cup placed inside an even larger
saucepan. Two waitresses ferried the courses to the tables. If you
wanted a cold beer, you had to wait until the trains stopped at one
of the stations that had a bar; there was no means of keeping ale
cold on the train.

*Pass through Sydney's Central station these and wanting food and the offerings
include burgers and fries. Back in 1924 the Soda Fountain near the main
departure platforms was staffed by assistants in smart and pressed uniforms
offering quick snacks and a range of drinks.* State Records NSW.

Dining cars did run on some of the more important expresses but, for the average rail traveller, the only option was the ubiquitous refreshment room, which were part of all the main (and many minor) stations around Australia. In many instances, private operators ran these by way of a concession; eventually, the government railway departments took control. The running of these establishments had to be well-organised, the meals and snacks all prepared in advance. As the first traveller rushed in the door off the platform to the dining rooms, the staff would be ladling soup into bowls. At the snack counters, rows of cups would be lined up ready for filling with tea or coffee as passengers surged across the platform.

Many refreshment rooms provided set table meals (we would, perhaps, call them 'sit-down meals'). In South Australia in 1912, there were such dining rooms at Adelaide itself and also at Brinkworth, Murray Bridge, Port Wakefield, Riverton and Terowie. The operators of these rooms were required by SAR to provide linen napkins when they served soup, hot roasts (alternatively chops, sausages or cold meats), vegetables, bread, butter and cheese, marmalade and tea or coffee. Counter refreshments were available at secondary stations such as Kapunda or Peterborough (soup, pork chops, fresh milk, tea and potatoes being some of the items on the menu). The next grade down of refreshment room offered sandwiches, buns, soup, tea or coffee, local white wine and beer; at such smaller stations as Balaklava, Mount Barker and Naracoorte — even though the menu might be rudimentary — you could nevertheless buy a Havana cigar to enjoy on the train. Outer stations (Keith and Leigh Creek, for example) provided fruit stalls. Gradually, South Australian Railways took over management of the refreshment rooms. Later, there were gradual closures as services ended or food became available on board trains. However, in 1917, with the completion of the line between Port Augusta and Kalgoorlie, SAR converted the goods shed at Eurelia into a refreshment room for passengers making the long transcontinental journey. From 1929, SAR required a deposit on each piece of crockery taken outside their refreshment rooms.

South Australian Railways did allow some private concessions: the Nestle and Anglo-Swiss Condensed Milk Company from 1915 was charged one pound a year for each chocolate dispensing machine installed on platforms around the state from 1915.

There were fifty-two refreshment rooms spread over the New South Wales system. When the magnificent refreshment room opened in late 1884 at the important northern New South Wales junction of Werris Creek, it seated between forty and fifty people at dinner. The rooms were entered from the main platform by large double doors, inside of which an impressive cedar staircase provided access to bedrooms on the upper floor. The dining room itself had a large cedar counter along one side. For the staff, there was a scullery, pantries and a cellar as well as the main kitchen.

Junee, on the main rail line south from Sydney, had refreshment rooms that were just as grand. The main dining hall's ceiling was lined with kauri panels; the main counter was more than twelve metres in length and its top made of marble. A wide, polished cedar staircase led to a private dining room and bedrooms on the upper level. The refreshment rooms were extended in 1891 to cope with increasing rail traffic in the Riverina and, in 1918, the private contractors were dropped and all the staff became railway department employees; many of them were live-in staff as the rooms were operated for many hours a day. However by the 1950s, as more and more passengers switched to road or air transport, vending machines were installed on the platforms. The glory days of the Junee refreshment rooms ended in the 1960s when dining and buffet cars were attached to trains.

Junee's refreshment rooms had a ceiling lined with kauri (a now rare New Zealand hardwood) panels. The main counter was more than twelve metres long and with a marble top. A wide, polished cedar staircase led to the private dining room and bedrooms on the upper level. This photograph dates from 1950; the refreshment rooms had only another decade before their role was usurped by dining cars being attached to major trains. State Records NSW.

The railway refreshment room at Coffs Harbour laid claim to having the best food on the New South Wales north coast. The fish was cooked in a locally devised batter; it was usually leather jacket but special occasions could see snapper or pearl perch being served. The dining room could seat 127, and there was also a counter servery for snacks and drinks. During the years of the Second World War, more than 100 people were employed at the rooms to cover all the shifts needed to cater for troop trains, each carrying up to three hundred men; as many as forty young women could be employed on a single shift to handle all the preparation and serving of sandwiches. Some 300 meat pies were baked each morning. After the war, when traffic was back to normal, the first public train each day was the Brisbane Express making its way south to Sydney, whose passengers could expect a traditional cooked breakfast at Coffs Harbour. This train was followed throughout the day by five more passenger workings.

The Depression of the 1930s apparently took its economic toll even on railway refreshment rooms. Staff throughout the South Australian railway system were exhorted to eat in them wherever possible to help bolster the takings; then in 1934 the price of luncheon or dinner in country refreshment rooms was reduced from two and sixpence to two shillings. But it was too late to save some and refreshment rooms started to close, a process that was to continue for several decades: Burra shut in 1936, Euralia the following year, and Terowie in 1939. Gladstone and Alawoona fell victims in 1967, Murray Bridge as late as 1973.

The 1937 timetable for Western Australian Government Railways (WAGR) reported that set meals could be obtained from the refreshment rooms located at Perth, Beverley, Wagin, Mount Barker, Fremantle, Pinjarra, Caron, Mullewa and Yalgoo. The timetable for daily passenger services each way on the Albany line saw Train No. 7 and Train No. 8 arrive at Wagin at the same time. The refreshment stall was located on the island platform, and its staff rushed to meet the needs of two trainloads of passengers simultaneously converging on them.

The WAGR had a refreshment factory at Welshpool, on the suburban line to Armadale, which produced various types of cakes and the famous railway pies. These were carried in refrigerated vans attached to passenger trains for delivery to the various refreshment rooms along the way. For those travelling from Perth to Kalgoorlie, for example, there were stalls located at Northam, Cunderdin, Merredin and Southern Cross stations, with main meals available in the dining cars attached to the trains. At many other stations, passengers made their own arrangements; at the almost deserted stations at Bullabulling and Karalee, for example, the train's stop was long enough to allow passengers to make a mad scramble for the small pubs at either place to slake their thirsts.

Mavis Shaw was, for a period after the Second World War, the cook at Mullewa station on the line inland from Geraldton to Meekatharra and Wiluna in Western Australia. The refreshment rooms were run by the manager and his wife; there was one full-time employee and another three who worked part-time on train days. Mrs Shaw would make the pies and pastries the day before trains were coming. On train days themselves, she prepared three-course meals and waited on tables. The guards would telephone from the preceding station and alert the manager to the number of meals that would be required when the train arrived. At night-time, she cooked for the single men employed on the railway who were based at Mullewa. There was also a tea bar, which served the pies along with sandwiches, tea and coffee, and a liquor bar (which also was known to provide an unofficial take-home supply service to the locals). Dolores Bone went to work at the newsagency at

Mullewa in 1946 when she was fourteen years old. As part of her duties, she would go to the station on the days when the trains to and from Wiluna were coming through to open the news stall on the platform, selling newspapers, magazines, tobacco and cigarettes to travellers.

Around 1900, the traveller on Victorian Railways was well provided for by way of refreshments. Thirteen stations had a set-table meal service. These ranged from Spencer Street in Melbourne to the border crossing at Serviceton. The refreshment rooms had opened at Serviceton on the border with South Australia in 1889, and passengers had time to take a relatively leisurely meal while locomotives from one colonial system were being uncoupled and replaced with those of the other. A menu dating from its first years showed the passengers could choose from soup, fish, hot joints (beef, lamb, mutton or pork), with vegetables (potatoes, parsnips, carrots and beans). Bread, butter, cheese and marmalade were provided, washed down by South Australian wine, or tea or coffee. The price was two shillings and sixpence. A further twenty-one stations provided counter refreshments, but even at these stations there was a robust choice: Irish stew, sausages, Victorian ale or claret by the half-pint, tea at three pence a cup, and ham sandwiches at sixpence. A 'Havannah' cigar set one back another sixpence. In the 1920s, more than five hundred young women were employed throughout the Victorian refreshments service. Victorian Railways had its own poultry farm to provide eggs and chickens for the refreshment rooms and, later, the dining cars.

The Clapp era in Victoria — the years when Harold Clapp was Commissioner of Railways — saw an unusual development on the platforms of some stations in that system: stalls selling fresh, healthy food such as vegetables, raisins, fruit juice and cheese. Clapp had posters erected extolling the virtues of eating fruit and then supplied the stalls where travellers could follow up on that advice. But the effort was not just intended to improve public health; Clapp wanted to help the farmers sell their produce at a time when rural incomes were shrinking. From 1926, for the price of four pence, you could buy a glass of juice squeezed while you waited.

However, there was one significant drawback to refreshment rooms: they meant that trains had to wait seven minutes or more while all the passengers were served. In 1934, Victorian Railways decided to introduce buffet cars on country lines to eliminate these time-consuming stops.

6

Building and Mending

THE RAILWAY WORKSHOPS WERE, in many ways, the very heart of the railway systems. They not only built many of the locomotives, wagons and carriages, but them kept them in working order. The two most impressive were Eveleigh in Sydney and Newport at North Melbourne, the latter opening in 1888. Workshops at Jolimont, Ballarat and Bendigo were all brought into operation in 1917.

The Eveleigh railway workshops in Sydney were built between 1880 and 1886, and lasted more than a century (until 1989). They incorporated huge running sheds where all the main line steam locomotives operating out of Sydney were serviced, along with the small local train and shunting engines. They achieved pre-eminence from 1889, once the completion of the bridge over the Hawkesbury River enabled rolling stock to be taken from depots in the northern part of the state for servicing in Sydney; as a result, thereafter the Newcastle workshops declined in importance. In 1939, the representative of the Australian Railway Union wrote this description of the Eveleigh works:

Row upon row of drab smoked-grimed buildings, housing a throbbing energy which pulses forth to the accompaniment of the thump, thump, thump of giant presses torturing white-hot steel into servitude. That is Eveleigh workshops, the heart of the state's transport system. There is a steady drone of high-powered machinery, drilling, boring and turning in every possible fashion; the clatter of overhead cranes, hurrying and scurrying, fetching and carrying, and the staccato noise of the boilermakers' rattler. Somehow this all resolved into a unity of sound. Disturbed only by an occasional burst of excessive violence from any one part. Seemingly submerged in this medley is the human element — 2,600 individuals, the strongest of them but puny weaklings besides the machines they control. Yet they make all possible. Without them the roaring giant would be a whispering ghost.

In 1971, there were still 1,648 people on the payroll at Eveleigh. Other notable workshops were those at Ipswich and Townsville in Queensland, Islington near Adelaide, Midland (both the government and Midland company had their plants there), and Launceston in Tasmania.

Queensland had to have more than one workshop system simply because for many decades it operated isolated sections based on the ports at Brisbane, Rockhampton and Townsville. For the Brisbane-based system, the first railway workshops were opened in Ipswich in 1865, and these began building wagons and other rolling stock right from their inception. The shops soon had to move to a bigger site and, over the years, evolved into a large industrial complex with about fifty separate buildings. It had its own powerhouse and sawmill. During the steam era, Ipswich turned out more than 200 new steam locomotives.

Another job well done — a key moment in the construction of a steam locomotive at Sydney's Eveleigh workshops. Here the frame and smoke box are lowered on to the bogies. Locomotive C3806 entered service on 29 November 1945. Steam-hauled passenger trains survived on New South Wales rails until 24 July 1971. State Records NSW.

Victoria built satellite workshops in various locations, notably at Ballarat and Bendigo. South Australia had a large workshop complex at Peterborough. While New South Wales had a policy of importing locomotives up until federation, Victoria decided it would manufacture as many as it could or buy locally. South Australia also played a role in locomotive building. William Thaw, who went on to be chief mechanical engineer with New South Wales Government Railways, designed the R class 4-6-0 machine during his time in Adelaide, which formed the basis of the New South Wales P class. E. E. Lucy, who followed Thaw as the chief mechanical engineer in Sydney, was a noted designer: he was responsible for the NN class first built in 1914.

Railway workshops played an important role during the two world wars with their equipment and manpower being harnessed to make weaponry. Indeed, this work took priority over the normal rolling stock work. In Victoria, Newport workshops were a vital part of the war effort in both conflicts. Between 1914 and 1918, the works manufactured high explosive and shrapnel shells; in the second war, Newport built 1,364 fuselages for Beaufort fighter bombers and the hulls for eight ocean-going tug boats.

The private sector played as important a part in the development of rolling stock. The Phoenix Foundry at Ballarat was founded in 1855 and was producing locomotives for Victorian Railways from 1873. In all, the foundry produced 351 railway engines. The first was Victorian Railways' No. 83, a 0-6-0, and among the classes produced were the Q, with their elegant green painted domes, along with the K and U classes. While Phoenix largely adapted designs from Beyer Peacock in Britain, the company did not import any prototypes and did all the final design work in Ballarat. From 1905, the government's Newport workshops took over all locomotive construction and by 1906 Phoenix was out of business.

Victoria Foundry, also in Ballarat, built Victorian Railways' first locomotive. It went on to make another 200 or so, some for railway departments in other Australian colonies.

In Queensland, there was Walkers Limited. The company built its first locomotive in 1873, a vertical boiler 0-4-0, 3 ft 3 in gauge engine for a tramway near Gympie. By the outbreak of the First World War, Walkers were turning out a locomotive a week. Walkers successfully made the switch into diesel and diesel–electric locomotive building in the 1950s.

Clyde Engineering (formerly Hudson Brothers) was one of the mainstays of rolling stock construction in New South Wales. A highlight of its history was the agreement with General Electric in 1949 — the first done by GE with a company outside the United States — to make the American company's locomotives under licence. It thereafter became an exporter to Asia, New Zealand and the Pacific. In October 1970, Clyde Engineering had on its order books eighteen diesel-electric locomotives for Commonwealth Railways, six X class for Victorian Railways, and one diesel-hydraulic engine for a Queensland sugar mill.

7

Working on the Railway

WE DO NOT KNOW her first name, but Mrs Ruttley was just one of many to find that things were tough if you were working in the railways, especially in the New South Wales Government Railways. Her plight came to the attention of the Australian Railway Union in 1935. Mrs Ruttley was working as a gatekeeper at Woy Woy, just north of Sydney, a task that involved closing gates at level crossings to stop road traffic as trains approached. She was not a member of the union, but we can probably presume her late husband had been. Most women gatekeepers were either the widows of railwaymen who had died while still in service, or who had been killed in a work accident, or were the wives of surviving workers who had been maimed at work. These women worked very long hours for appalling pay. The union newspaper, *Railroad*, reported that some did second jobs, like taking in washing, to make ends meet. Mrs Ruttley was the sole support for three children.

The union newspaper reported that Mrs Ruttley had been to the doctor who found her to be on verge of a nervous breakdown due to the excessive hours she was required to be on duty. The union discovered that Mrs Ruttley was working 117 hours and fourteen minutes a week, including an unbroken thirty-six hours from 6.00 am on Sunday until 6.00 pm on Monday. She was paid

The final 472 km section of the Central Australia Railway, the section between Oodnadatta and Alice Springs, was opened for traffic on 2 August 1929. This section, as can be seen, was laid with the minimum of formation and a great deal of hard physical labour. The men, who have just dropped a rail section on to the sleepers, have their hands protected by binding: the steel would have been very hot in the middle of a blazing day in centre of Australia. Northern Territory Archives

ten shillings and ten pence a week, plus eight shillings and one penny in lieu of quarters being provided. Tax took one shilling and eleven pence. Even by 1935 standards, this was clearly inadequate when rent, food and clothing for herself and three children had to be found. The union's efforts resulted in Mrs Ruttley's hours being reduced to eighty-eight a week, with a relief gatekeeper provided on Sundays and Mondays. Yet, even in the 1940s, there was a Mrs Gleason who was gatekeeper at the Darling Street crossing at Dubbo: on some days, she was required to be available to work the gates for up to twenty-two hours a day.

A gatekeeper's house at Jubilee Lake on the Daylesford line in Victoria. The gatekeeper, Mrs Liversidge, is leaning against the gate, the others presumably being members of her family. Merle Reiffel collection.

Railway work was hard work at many levels. Steam locomotives needed to be fired by hand; most freight was loaded and unloaded by men unaided by any machinery; track building and repair was, by and large, backbreaking work; and gates at level crossings had to be opened and closed by gatekeepers. It seems extraordinary that, as late as the 1960s, some railway workers in New South Wales were still expected to live in tents.

The railways employed vast numbers of people — 30,202 on the payroll of Victorian Railways alone in 1952 (and surprising in that road transport had already made huge inroads on the railway's business). And railway work was both labour-intensive and largely self-supporting: Victorian Railways, for example, had an ice works in its main Melbourne yard until the 1980s which supplied ice for the insulated wagons carrying perishable goods. There was also a nursery on the Upfield line in Melbourne to provide plants to beautify stations around the state. Victorian Railways' own bakery pioneered the production of raisin bread in the state, both for its own use and for sale to the public. But Victorian Railways' aegis extended far beyond railways. In 1888, the Minister of Railways was given the added responsibility of developing tourism in the colony (using the railway system, of course). This role was further extended in 1924 when the railways department took over the Mt Buffalo Chalet and other alpine resorts.

Not just a chalet, but also a coal mine. In 1909, the Victorian government opened the state coal mine at Wonthaggi. This was precipitated by a strike at the Hunter Valley coal fields in New South Wales, hitherto the source of coal for Victoria's large steam locomotive fleet. In the early days of the strike there was no option but to fuel the locomotives with wood once shipments from Newcastle ceased; as an interim measure, coal was imported from India and Japan while the authorities in Melbourne hurried plans for the state's own mine (the first state-owned coal operation in Australia).

The Wonthaggi deposits were not popular with Victorian Railways engine crews; the coal was poor, friable and of low calorific value in terms of steam locomotive purposes and was notorious for clinkering or choking the fires. By 1910, the mine was in full production, although the coal had to be hauled by road to Nyora — the nearest railway station — until a branch was laid to the mine. Because the bulk of the coal was going for railway use, the government passed control of the mine to VR in July 1911. The operation continued until 1968, the switch to diesel traction being well under way by that time.

Queensland Railways in the 1890s employed the drivers, firemen, guards, porters, gangers — but that same department had people on the payroll like John Wooley, paid eight shillings a week as a washoutman; he got inside boilers of steam locomotives to clean them. Then there were staff classified as tarrers, land valuators, pumpers, mounted messengers, waiting room attendants, tracers, polishers, sawyers, station gardeners, cement testers, iron bridge inspectors, spring makers, lad porters and cleaners and the ubiquitous lengthsmen — those men posted to various main and remote stations who were responsible for the maintenance of a specified section of line. In 1936, Queensland Railways advertised the position of 'Porter in charge and caretaker of bores, Dajarra'; the successful applicant would have a knowledge of steam pumping plants, deep well pumps and internal combustion engines — and would hold a 3rd Class ticket. A house and fuel were provided along with the weekly pay of £6.13.7d.

In the 1920s, one Les Potts was assigned to the Western line as a steam fitter to maintain all the pumping stations out toward Charleville and branch lines. He travelled in a van marked

'Water Supply Fitter', which would be attached to trains as needed. The car had a sleeping bunk, wood stove, water tank, and kerosene lighting. It carried every piece of equipment needed to maintain the pumps that lifted water into the tanks that supplied steam locomotives. Queensland Railways, at one point, was that state's largest employer and it certainly accounted for a large slice of Queensland's yearly apprentice intake.

New South Wales Government Railways operated a number of gasworks to supply lighting for stations, yards and locomotive and goods sheds. Such gasworks existed at Sydney (run by a Gas Superintendent), Junee, Bathurst, Newcastle and Werris Creek. At Sydney's second plant, located by the Eveleigh carriage shed, there were pipes laid to convey the gas to the then Sydney station at Redfern, which was then compressed and pumped into cylinders slung on the underside of the carriages, this providing the fuel for the gas lighting for passengers. It has been recorded that smells from the burning of coal and the use of chemicals made railway gasworks very unpleasant places to work. Gas was gradually replaced by electric lighting, both at stations and in carriages.

Many of the jobs, although poorly paid, required men employed by the railway departments to develop considerable levels of skills or responsibility. There were, in 1926, twenty-nine men employed by Victorian Railways at the North Melbourne locomotive depot coal stage. One of them was designated 'fuelman'. His job required him to keep records of all trucks removing ash; to load the stage daily placing different types of coal in various places within the coal stage, to instruct shunters what coal to put up to a locomotive, to check that engines were allocated the correct type of coal, to take coal samples for laboratory testing, to check tickets for wagons discharged by the coal labourers, to oversee the bagging of difference types of coals for other depots, to assist checking all fuel dockets and to trim the footboards of the coal stage itself. The railway departments saw themselves as a world apart, as vast organisations reaching into every part of their respective states, and their staff members all playing their parts in that these vast enterprises. The 1928 Victorian Railways suburban timetable contained this panel called 'The Porter's Job':

> The work of the private soldier is as essential to victory as the work of a general. The Railway Porter is one of the private soldiers of the railway army. His duty to you is to render assistance and information in transacting railway business and help you personally with your luggage and parcels so far as his station duties and his duties to other passengers permit. He is especially instructed to help the aged and the infirm, and ladies with young children, and to give you sympathetic attention should your luggage go astray.

Life was tough and hard for many railway workers. And not just for the men (and their wives) who lived at remote locations. Being chief civil engineer on Commonwealth Railways was a senior and important job; but it was also an arduous one as late as the 1950s mainly because so much of the track operated by CR was laid across the barren Nullabor Plain; rushing to the sites of washouts and derailments along the Nullarbor route was part of the job. The chief civil engineer carried a swag like the rest of his crew, dossed in wire stretchers at rest huts along the line — huts with no fans, electric light or refrigeration. Meat was kept in a box made of perforated zinc and there was water only if there had been rain and it had been collected in the tank attached to a roof downpipe.

In the 1960s, the rail magazine *Bulletin* recorded the memories of Percy Budden, an engine driver who had retired from New

South Wales Government Railways in 1942 (he had begun his employment in 1901 at Murrurundi as an engine cleaner). Mr Budden recalled being a relief fireman on the Warren branch in 1914, which required the crew to use the railway barracks at the Warren terminus on trips from Nevertire. There was no entertainment and the barracks hut in which the three men stayed was built under the locomotive water tank and consisted of one bedroom, and a small cooking area. On Sundays, the railwaymen's only day off, they would wait until the local Aboriginals had had their daily swim in the local waterhole — naked, of course — and then the three NSWGR men would get in the waterhole, fully dressed. This would allow them to wash their working clothes which, after returning to the barracks, they would take off and drape over trees to allow the gear to dry.

Men employed at larger stations had clearly defined areas of work. At the smaller stations, you were expected to be jacks-of-all-trades. Viv Arnott, who had started as a junior porter at Tumbarumba in 1948, was in 1950 assigned to Finley in the New South Wales region of Riverina. He never found much spare time in his daily shift that lasted from 8.00 am until 5.00 pm. His duties included cleaning the station lavatories, waxing and polishing the station counter, putting Brasso on the taps, sweeping the platform, cutting the hedges around the station, delivering goods and parcels to local homes and businesses, filling up the signal lamps with kerosene — and keeping the signal lights clean. There was no shunting engine available at Finley, so he would use a crowbar under a wheel to move a sheep wagon along the siding to the loading race. In fact, on days when livestock was due to be railed out, Viv Arnott had to be out of bed at 4·00 am.

But that was uncomplicated compared to the activities at the main stations. Victorian Railways in the 1920s employed sixty-nine first class goods checkers and 140 second class ones. Most were assigned to Melbourne, but with smaller numbers at Ballarat, Bendigo and Geelong. Their job was to ensure that each of the many thousands of items that passed through the depot each day made it to the correct station. Each station had its individual mark or brand.

And there was always plenty of paperwork — usually in the form of notices from head office, giving details of special trains and, more often, laying down the law. On 1 June 1916 the weekly notice in Queensland Railways included the following stricture: 'Recently a corpse was conveyed in the dogbox of a guard's van. This must not be permitted on any account. When a mortuary box is not available a box wagon must be specially provided'.

Near the bottom of the heap were the call boys. At Dubbo in 1940 Allen Gordon was one of three call boys employed at the locomotive depot. The senior boy assisted the roster clerk while the two others worked either the day or night shifts. The day boy would ride around Dubbo on a pushbike to advise drivers firemen and shed staff of their next rostered duty or to deliver any message sent by the charge man or the roster clerk. The night call boy would go around to the homes of the engine crew members and give them a wake-up call one hour before they were due on duty. Before finishing at 6.30am, the boy would wash the station floors.

Marriages were frequent events between railway employees. Such was the case with Terry Thiele who in 1939 was sent as a fifteen-year-old to Adelaide to sit an examination, a test required before he could become a junior porter with South Australian Railways. He passed and was assigned to Alawoona to learn how to handle parcels and paperwork. At the age of eighteen he sat another examination to become an assistant guard. Subsequently he worked his way up to fireman, and then driver, until he met Corallie, his future wife, who was working in the refreshment rooms. So he could be home more often, Terry switched over to the refreshments branch and ended up running the Murray Bridge rooms with a staff of twenty-seven. The day began there at 4.30 am in time for the arrival an hour later of the Blue Lake, the train operating between Mount Gambier and Adelaide. No soon had the rooms emptied and the Blue Lake departed than, at 6.00 am, the Overland from Melbourne slid into the station, the passengers offered a sit-down breakfast before they reboarded the train and continued on to Adelaide. The day's work ended at 9.00 pm after the Melbourne-band Overland had departed eastwards. Shifts started at 4.30 am and 12.30 pm and there was always a waiting list of people wanting jobs there.

Not that working in refreshment rooms was always an attractive job. Rosemary Webb, in her study *A Refreshing Advance* for the Labour Council of Australia of New South Wales, where she investigated conditions during the 1920s and 1930s, found the job of working in a refreshment room had been arduous and hard, especially for the women. At Yass in 1924 members of staff had to sleep in tents. There were also accidents: a Madge Moodie, working at Sydney Terminal, lost most of a finger when using a bread slicer. Costs of breakages were often deducted from wages. The New South Wales women were required to work split shifts and late shifts but, in Sydney, the department refused to reinstate free late-night tram travel for the women to get home.

Few refreshment employees were on permanent staff. At country stations the rooms were often operated by married couples acting as sub-managers. There were other pressures: the manager at Molong refreshment rooms tried to stop staff joining the Australian Railways Union. Females employed in the wine bar at Sydney station had to fight to be paid the barmaids' minimum wage. Women could be sacked at any time, so job security was tenuous.

Lloyd Ross of the NSW division of the Australian Railways Union was a steadfast campaigner for better conditions in the refreshment rooms. One case that stood out was that of two counter-hands at a country station whose eight-hour working day was spread over twenty-one hours: they began work at 2.30 am, taking a break at 4.30 am; they had to be back behind the counter from 7.00 am until 8.30 am, then again between 9.00 am and 11.30 am. The afternoon and early evening were free but then the women were expected to clock on from 9.30 pm until 11.00 pm.

In 1938 the union won, with a new award redressing the more oppressive of the working conditions. Hours were limited to forty hours a week or eighty hours spread over a fortnight. Women at the main Sydney stations would work only seventy-two hours a fortnight. Nevertheless, the wage differentials were substantial. The male chef at Wynyard (an inner city Sydney underground station) was paid £7.3s.0d a week and even the third male cook would get £5.0s.6d. But a 'female cook alone' at a station where only one meal a day was served could expect a basic £2.19s.6d a week. Kitchen men were worth £4.0.6d but kitchen maids £2.10s.6d.

Ross also campaigned for the men, especially those with the more dangerous jobs; and nothing was more dangerous than the work of a shunter. These men had constantly to be on their toes as locomotives accelerated quickly and then braked hard, propelling an uncoupled wagon or set of wagons on to various sidings to make up trains going to various destinations. The shunter was required to throw points to ensure each wagon went to the correct train being assembled, and then attach the couplings after the wagon had slammed into its train. Mary Matthews, who spent her childhood in a railway family posted to various parts of New South Wales, remembers that it was her grandfather's death while working as a shunter at the northern New South Wales station of Mungindi that led to the introduction of more widespread first aid training. Her grandfather, Andrew Murphy, had been badly injured on 23 February 1923. This small item appeared in the *Sydney Morning Herald* the next day:

> Andrew Murphy, a railway guard, residing at Narrabri with his wife and three children, met with a fatal accident this morning in Mungindi railway yards while shunting. In attempting to come from between trucks he was struck by a wheel, which passed over his leg. He was taken to the local hospital, but died from shock and loss of blood.

Murphy was still alive after the accident but he bled to death because no one at the station knew first aid. As was often the case in such circumstances, the widow, Lulu, was offered a job cleaning the railway barracks at Tottenham, the terminus of the eponymous branch line.

Four shunters died on New South Wales railways in the first six months of 1938. This was not an unusual statistic for the times but became news because Ross organised strikes and stoppages over the issue and even led a delegation to the office of the chief commissioner. The appearance of blue-collar workers in the chief commissioner's office was unheard of until this incident. Mark Hearn, who chronicled the history of the New South Wales branch of the Australian Railways Union, cites one of the 1938 cases. Timm Stephen Dwyer, aged forty-one, had been crushed between two wagons in the Enfield yard in Sydney. This marshalling yard contained more than 160 km of track, with the yard sloping downhill so making it possible to shunt wagons simply by allowing gravity to take over after an initial shove by the locomotive. Timm Dwyer was managing a rake of fifty-six wagons. A set of couplings on one of the wagons was defective, so he got into between that and another wagon, being crushed to death in the process. After the strikes and the deputation, the railways department agreed to increasing staff numbers in the goods yards, and reducing working hours. And, as Hearn recorded, the shunters were at last issued with gloves, no longer having to grapple bare-handed with the couplings.

This picture is not dated but the Enfield yards would have been little changed from the day Timm Dwyer was killed there in a shunting accident. The photo shows a selection of rolling stock. Note the elegant light fittings to allow night shunting. State Records NSW.

While women who worked in the various railway systems found that they were usually at the low end of the pay scale and sometimes subject to exploitation, they did play a very important role in keeping the trains running and stations operating. Many women were employed as station mistresses — they were often wives of railwaymen who were given small payments and also exemption of rents on railway houses for looking after smaller country stations (of which, more later). At the other end were those unpaid women, the wives of construction workers or fettlers or pumpers who often lived in remote places with rudimentary housing and few amenities and where there were no small, extra jobs for wives. In between, there were all types of roles for women. At the tiny station of Crowther in the central west of New South Wales, one fettler and his wife were given a departmental house next to the level crossing at the station. Until 1937, the fettler's wife was paid a small amount to operate the gates that had to be closed across the road when a train was approaching. This woman also, from a small room attached to the house, operated the Crowther post office and manual telephone exchange. (One of the fettlers, meanwhile, was paid an extra allowance to remove the night soil from the men's lavatory at the station.)

William (Bill) Archibald and Ivy Victoria Wilson were married on 10 April 1926, having met at the Victorian Railway Institute dance above the Flinders Street station in Melbourne. Bill's address on the marriage certificate was 'Railway Rest Home, Ouyen', the remote station in the Mallee region where he was a fettler, the Mallee being typified by a monotonous landscape broken by sand dunes. Ivy, who had lived at her sister's substantial home in suburban Melbourne with all the modern conveniences of the time, now faced life in Ouyen with the storms that deposited red

Mallee dust throughout the house even when all the doors and windows were shut.

Within a few months, though, the Wilsons managed to get themselves transferred to the more comfortable siding of Sailors Falls on the Daylesford line in central Victoria. Ivy's daughter, Merle Reiffel, remembers her mother distributing mail and selling passenger tickets.

Then it was a move to Tylden, further along the same line. Bill was employed as a line repairer and Ivy as gatekeeper, and they were provided with a four-bedroom railway house. The gates were normally left open to road traffic at night, there being no train services; on public holidays, the routine was the opposite with the gates being closed to road traffic all night (one New Year's Day saw nineteen trains pass the station) so that any motorist wanting to cross the line would have to toot his horn until someone got out of bed and opened the gates.

In dry spells, Bill would arrange for a goods train to hook up a water wagon and stop and pump water into the station tank. The main contact with the outside world was the *Sun News-Pictorial* newspaper from Melbourne which was thrown off by crews of passing trains. Merle Reiffel recalls that, when some of the wooden boards on a wall had rotted away, Victorian Railways solved the problem by having nailed to the wall iron sheets which, of course, made the small house a furnace on hot summer days. But the worst part of having a railway house was the departmental inspection. It was, she recalls, 'tension time'. Merle remembers the inspectors arriving in a Dodge touring car that had been converted to run on rails. Her mother always kept the house clean, the lamps polished, just in case she suddenly heard the car approaching. As Merle recalls, everything belonging to the Victorian Railways was marked with a crow's-foot with a 'V' on the left and an 'R' on the right of it. Dad was issued with a VR shovel, pick and crowbar. All these items had to stand in a row in the backyard by the gate which opened out on to the railway line. Cutlery and crockery used on the trains was also marked and the commissioners came into the house and looked in the drawers and cupboards to see that none of these items had been taken for our own use.

It seems that, in country Australia, the fettlers and their families fitted in with the locals, even though they often were assigned to places for only a year or two. Merle Reiffel says that her father cleaned the local hall before dances; on one occasion, when the booked musicians failed to turn up, Bill got on his trolley and drove along the line to fetch a local who could play the accordion. The children were welcome in local houses, going everyday to a farming family nearby.

But there was also an 'informal economy' side of railway life, to use modern terminology, within the railways. Such was the case with a Mrs Muller who lived at Orallo, the intermediate station on Queensland's Injune branch at which the steam locomotives took on water, hence involving a long stop while that was taking place. When the thrice-weekly train left Injune in the 1920s for its return to Roma on the Western line, the station mistress would call her counterpart at Orallo and indicate how many people were travelling and would be expecting to be fed while the locomotive crew took on water, the head count then being passed on to Mrs Muller who ran Orallo's only store, which included the post office and telephone exchange; she was also the local midwife. Even though this first part of the journey covered only 52.6 km, the train took three hours to get to Orallo due to all the stops in between and a low speed limit (there would be another two and a half hours to go before Roma was reached). This gave Mrs Muller enough time to make sandwiches and cakes and then wheel them in an old pram to the station. She boiled the kettle on the platform and, for two shillings, a traveller could have a sandwich, a scone and a piece of fruit cake or sponge, along with as much tea as they could drink.

And then there were the wives who had no job but lived wherever the railway department sent their husbands. Before he became an assistant stationmaster at Binnaway in New South Wales, Lance Forlonge worked as a guard on trains to Dubbo, Werris Creek, Mudgee and Gwabegar. Sometimes he would be away from home for as long as thirty-six hours, much of the time spent in railway barracks waiting for a train to work back to Binnaway. His wife, Venessa, remembers it as a lonely life for women who had no family nearby. Sometimes the steam train crews would be at their home station for as little as eight hours before heading off across country again. Venessa remembers the never-ending job of packing tucker boxes so that Lance would have something to eat when he stayed overnight away from home. That meant making sandwiches and cakes, and packing biscuits, meat, fruit and vegetables, the quantity of the provisions depending on how long he was going to be away. One time Lance and his crew were stranded in Werris Creek for a week after a flood washed away the line.

On the other hand, she recalls, railway towns like Binnaway were close-knit communities and there was always someone to help in a crisis. And there were enough people to support sporting clubs, with a choice of golf, bowls, tennis, and football.

Everything in this photograph taken on 15 November 1952 is now but a distant memory. The near-new Garratt 6004, the MRC refrigerator van coupled behind the engine, then the CW cattle wagon and the RU wheat hopper wagons are long gone — as are the water columns at Tuggerah, New South Wales. State Records NSW.

The country stationmaster

At the main stations in the capital cities, there was a complex and inflexible hierarchy. Even below the top brass — the chief commissioner and other head office exalted types — these termini were ruled over by stationmaster and assistant stationmasters, along with district superintendents. This pecking order was replicated, to a more modest extent, at regional junctions. Everyone knew their place and discipline was tight, with regulations expected to be obeyed to the letter.

But, at the country station level, life was more informal. Ernie Thomas, who spent twenty-three years as stationmaster at Coolamon on the Hay branch line, found he often had to roll up his sleeves and help the yard staff. Coolamon had a stationmaster, assistant stationmaster and two station assistants. Ernie joined New South Wales Government Railways on 23 August 1949 as a junior porter at Murrumburrah. He served seven years as stationmaster at Coolah before being assigned to Coolamon. (His life thereafter was a comparatively settled one; a compiler of a listing of Victorian stationmasters found one man, who after being promoted to that level, had to shift stations seventeen times.)

Coolamon was always a busy station. Two chaff mills provided a constant flow of bags to be loaded on wagons at the siding, with the assistants kept occupied making sure the wagons were loaded, the bags covered by tarpaulins and the sheets tied down with ropes. Coolamon also had large quantities of wheat arriving to be railed out, but that was all handled by grain elevator staff. Ernie started his day about 7.45 am and already empty wagons would have been left at the station by overnight goods trains. Once a week covered wagons would arrive from Darling Harbour goods yards in Sydney with consignments for the local businesses, groceries and beer among the load. The overnight passenger train from Sydney brought ice cream packed in aluminium containers encased in green canvas bags filled with dry ice, and it was always one of the first items to be unloaded. At least three goods trains stopped at Coolamon each day, with additional trains during the wheat harvest. Drought time somewhere in New South Wales or Victoria would mean loading hay for transport to the afflicted region. In his early days at Coolamon, there were gates at the level crossing by the station which had to be closed across the road before each train. The stationmaster's job included supervising shunting, looking after parcels arriving or being consigned and issuing passenger tickets.

Two passenger trains a day stopped at Coolamon. The South West Mail from Sydney stopped at about 9.00 am and then passed through again at 8.00 pm on its return trip from Griffith. The Riverina Express ran through two days a week. A booking for the Riverina Express would mean a telephone call to Cootamundra, where the seating plan for that train was held. Otherwise, whether it be tickets for trains leaving Sydney, such as the Brisbane Express or the Indian Pacific, Sydney had to be called; if the prospective passenger was not in a hurry, Ernie would send a telegram rather than telephone.

Everything had to be accounted for by the stationmaster. If a consignment arrived from Darling Harbour with freight charges owing, the stationmaster had to ensure those were collected. Ernie said some railway employees tried to siphon off some of the money, but you never got away with it. The area inspectors visited twice a year and expected everything to be clean and in order, with brass polished. Any shortcomings would result in a severe reprimand. An auditor arrived once a year to go through the station accounts.

The stationmaster was the link with the local people. In 1929, *Victorian Railways Magazine* praised the work of a Mr A.F. Menhennitt, stationmaster at the eighth-class station of Kingston on the Daylesford line. The article's writer found astonishing the amount of revenue Kingston was generating considering the closeness of other stations on this cross-country railway. Allendale was 3.2 km along the line in one direction, Newlyn 5.2 km in the other. More than 12,000 tons of chaff and potatoes had been consigned at Kingston over the previous year — twenty-five wagon-loads of chaff a week and twelve of potatoes. The station was also holding its own on passenger numbers in the face of growing road competition. The magazine said the principle factor in all this was the untiring efforts of Mr Menhennitt, stationmaster for the preceding seven years. His popularity with the locals had kept traffic on the rail that could easily have been lost to the new wave of trucks on the roads. The magazine noted the clean and tidy station at Kingston and the fact that Mr Menhennitt also handled the money and banking for several other stations along the line — Leonards Hill, Wombat, Rocklyn, Newlyn and Allandale. 'With the willing assistance of Lad Porter J.A. Murray, the multitudinous details of the day-to-day life at the station passes off with a swing,' the magazine concluded.

At the bigger places along the rail systems, the stationmaster would have assistants. That was certainly the case at Binnaway in New South Wales where, when Lance Forlonge joined the railways in 1957 as a junior station assistant and would work his way up there to assistant stationmaster, the staff numbers went well over one hundred and fifty. There were twenty-five train crews — drivers, firemen and guards — some of whom lived in the forty-bed barracks at one end of the yard; then there were between sixty and seventy fettlers and their bosses (with at least twelve families, including children, living in tents in the railway yards). The locomotive depot, which could house up to eight engines, would have as many as fifteen labourers whose main task was to fuel the locomotives; before loading the coal by shovel, they would rake out ashes after engines had their fires cleaned (or dropped); one man was employed to operate the pump house on the banks of the Castlereagh River which had a steam pump to keep the overhead water vats full; Ruth Glen was employed on a forty-hour week to look after the rest house, or barracks, where crews from other depots would stay, and her task included stripping and remaking beds, washing sheets and pillowslips, and generally keeping the barracks clean; there were men to handle the freight, five shunters and several call boys whose job it was to cycle around town and tell drivers and firemen when they were needed; there was a roster clerk in the loco depot, a clerk in the station and — over all this — the stationmaster and his four assistant stationmasters (or ASMs as they were always known). The ASM's job was largely taken up supervising the train running, making sure the rosters for shunters and guards were done, calling guards at night when they were needed and supervising the shunting. When the station lost its clerk in 1960, the ASMs took on the task of selling tickets and doing the accounts.

Once a fortnight the pay car — a small, motorised rail bus — arrived at Binnaway. It had already stopped along the track to pay fettlers; at each station, the pay car would have envelopes of cash for every staff member, the money having been drawn from the bank at Werris Creek.

The station was on the east-west line between Werris Creek and Dubbo; another line came in from Sydney and Mudgee, and then there was the 145 km Gwabegar branch running off to the north. Over a twenty-four hour period, between twelve and twenty trains a day came through Binnaway. Stock trains ran through, but every other train was shunted at Binnaway. Trains would arrive from Gwabegar with as many as twenty wagons of cypress pine bound for Sydney. There were coal trains bound for Dubbo and Mudgee. Wheat, sleepers and wool filled other wagons. Mondays, Wednesdays and Fridays saw three passenger services arrive at Binnaway and then set off for their return journeys to Mudgee, Dubbo and Gwabegar. Parcels from Dubbo and Mudgee bound for the Gwabegar line would often overflow the goods storage space and would be stacked on passenger seats. The station staff worked flat-out for two hours transferring items between the three trains — general parcels, chickens, meat, bread, butter, milk, eggs, fish and ice cream containers. The Gwabegar train would drop parcels and perishables at various stations along the line.

Today, no railway workers are employed at Binnaway. The line to Gwabegar was closed in 2005.

You had to take the good with the bad if you wanted to attain the position of stationmaster. When the job of stationmaster at Brewarrina became vacant in 1902, William Knox was advised to apply. As his wife later wrote in her memoirs, 'he needed only two years in the west and then he would be in a position to obtain any good position offered'. Knox had previously been stationmaster at Woolbrook. The couple spent five years in Brewarrina and Cecilia Knox recorded they were pleased to get away at the end of that stint to Walcha and somewhere cooler.

The smallest stations may not have justified a stationmaster but they all needed someone to run them. Danyo was one such. Located on the Mallee line between Ouyen in Victoria to the South Australian border at Pinnaroo, Danyo station was essentially a platform standing between the only two buildings of the town — the store and attached house on one side of the line, the district hall on the other. In good seasons, the station was busy handling the produce of the farms, including those on the soldier settler bloc, that lay on either side of the railway line, with the Big Desert to the north.

Henry George Moorhouse ran the local store after giving up farming due to heart problems; he was also a buying agent for the big wheat exporters, including Bunge and W.S. Kimpton and Sons. Being the only person living near the station — the Moorhouse family lived in the house attached to the shop which also served as the post office and telephone exchange (his wife was the postmistress and exchange operator) — he was employed in the 1920s and 1930s by Victorian Railways as caretaker at Danyo. There was a small office on the platform from where he telephoned consignment details through to Cowangie down the line, which was a station with a stationmaster and porter. There was plenty for George to do: there were three trains a week in either direction (with specials added during the wheat harvest). Wheat, sheep, cream cans and mallee roots had to be loaded and details 'phoned through. His daughter, Fay Lucas, remembers the locals coming into the station on train day to collect their mail, or parts for their cars, as well as farm machinery and equipment. Wagons full of superphosphate were also dropped off the Danyo siding.

Once a year, Henry was given a railway pass to take his family on holiday to Melbourne. The Moorhouses joined the thrice-weekly train at Danyo about 3.00pm and then settled down for the slow trip over about 110 km to Ouyen where the carriage from the mixed train was attached to the Mildura Express. It took the Mallee train until after 9.30 pm to reach Ouyen, and Melbourne was not reached about 8.30 am the next day. Fay Lucas remembers the trip as seemingly endless, with shunting at every station and more time spent with the crew talking to the staff at the various stations.

The station mistress

Station mistresses were common through much of the Australian railway system. They were a means of staffing smaller stations without having to pay the full wage of a stationmaster; often the women so employed were married to railway workers or men who had some business with the railway. In the days when country stations sold small numbers of passenger tickets, or the goods operation would be confined to a few wagons a week, station mistresses were the answer. After all, someone had to make sure paperwork was filled out, mail delivered and passengers were given tickets for their journeys.

Dorothy May Tompson in 1935 became station mistress at the tiny branch line station of Kywong in New South Wales. In return for not paying the five shillings a week rent for the railway house, she met the three times a week train, filled out bills of lading as the farmers brought in their wheat or other produce, ordered wagons and tarpaulins from Junee and — most importantly — keep the department's house spotless, a requirement of her tenancy. Every so often, a wagon full of tarpaulins and ropes would be sent down with a train to Kywong to be used to cover wool, skins and hides being railed out (but quite a few ended up with the local farmers and carriers). She was provided with some home-wares, such as towels, but these were all embossed with the New South Wales Government Railways crest and had to be accounted for. Dorothy's husband was a former railway carpenter whose job was managing the wheat silos at Kywong.

Maria Morgan was the wife of a ganger in Victoria who became station mistress at Trawool; she was the only employee at the station although down the line lived a gatekeeper who patrolled the level crossing and made ends meet by growing a little wheat and keeping cows on railway land. Maria's railway house was lit by kerosene lamps and candles. Her husband, Edward, had been transferred from Caithkin in about 1918. Edward, a track repairer or fettler, was paid £3.10s.0d a fortnight while Maria earned £1.5s.0d as station mistress. The family also had the mail contract which involved carrying the post bag off the morning train, up to the village's post office, and then collecting the outward mail at the end of the day to be sent out on the late train. Maria was also responsible for reading the river gauge. Summer was a busy time at Trawool station as holiday-makers arrived from

Melbourne and spread out alongside the banks of the Goulburn River. Edward and Maria's seven children were able to make some pocket money by selling fresh mushrooms to people arriving on the trains. One daughter, Jean Kirwan, remembers the annual visit of the Chief Commissioner of Victorian Railways, Harold Clapp, when all the local children were let out of school to see his special railway carriage pass through Trawool.

They usually knew their business, did the station mistresses.

Gertie Bradley, in charge of Tylden station in Victoria in 1898 certainly did. She was helping the guard load parcels into the brake van of the afternoon train from Daylesford when she heard a rumbling noise back up the track whence the passenger train had come on its way to Woodend. After the train had left Fern Hill — on its way to stopping at Tylden — two wagons had run away down the line. There was no telephone communication between the two stations so Tylden was not aware of the impending disaster, and a disaster it would have been with two rail wagons out of control and smashing into the rear of the stationary passenger working. But Mrs Bradley realised what that rumble was — and got everyone out of the train before the guard's van and other vehicles were smashed almost to pieces by the impact. For that 'commendable promptitude' as the department termed it, Gertie Bradley was awarded a special payment of five pounds.

The signalman

On 28 August 1942, Dick Clarke was appointed to Warrungen, a new loop built by New South Wales Government Railways between Tamworth and Armidale to speed up traffic on the Main North Line which had become even busier than in pre-war times due to the increasing numbers of troop trains. His wife Jean (they had married only the preceding May) remembered it as the outstanding part of their 'railway life' together. Dick, who had spent two years training in the militia with the 56th Battalion, had applied to join the army but was turned down on the grounds he was involved in essential work.

Warrungen was located just over 60 km north of Tamworth; the nearest station, Woolbrook, was about 6 km away. The Clarkes arrived to find nothing in place and barely a structure in sight. They could see a shearers' hut, while the one unoccupied house near that hut had been snapped up by George Waters who had already arrived to work at Warrungen. George and Dick were appointed signalmen to provide between them coverage over twenty-four hours each day.

Each worked at least ten hours a day to provide close to around-the-clock attendance at the signal box; the working days had to be flexible to fit in with timetabled trains using the loop. They had a small signal box, just large enough to accommodate one man at a time, and three signal levers; but there were no point switches at the box, the men having to walk to the points at either when those switches needed to be thrown.

The railway department had promised there were to be cabins brought to the loop for the two married couples, but these had not arrived. Dick, through the stationmaster at Woolbrook, found a house to rent near that township. A local bachelor owned it and Jean and her young brother had to spend two days cleaning to make the place liveable. For Dick, getting to work meant riding his push bike over a rough track back and forth with each shift. The department meanwhile brought in two tents joined by a tarpaulin. There was a wooden floor and wooden sides that came halfway up inside the tents. At the edge of the tarpaulin there was an open fireplace; it had steel supports with bars across the fire from which to hang billies or a camp-oven. A hole was dug and a timber lavatory placed over it; this latter was portable and could be moved to replacement pits as needed. The only telephone was one linked to stations either side, so the two couples had no access to a public telephone.

Jean suggested that she and Dick move into the tents until the cabins arrived to save her husband those arduous bicycle rides each day. So they shifted out of their newly cleaned house, hiring a small truck to take their belongings to their new tent home. Carpet squares on the wooden boards made the place look a bit more comfortable. But the new bed sheets were soon stained by rust through having to boil them up in kerosene tins hung over the fire, an especial hardship since wartime rationing made linen goods prized and not easily replaced. But the Clarkes soon found themselves part of the community. Dick helped one local farmer with mustering for the shearing during shifts while Jean helped in the farmhouse kitchen; in return, there was a ready supply of milk and eggs available.

By December, though, the heat was starting to make tent life unbearable. So they moved into the shearers' hut, which consisted of three living rooms and bathroom — but none of the rooms was connected, so each had to be accessed from the exterior of the structure. Again, the carpet squares made the place homely. That Christmas, Jean's parents came up from Cooma by train. On the big day, the meat was discovered to be fly-blown and then the plum pudding swelled beyond the size of the boiler pot and burned out the bottom of the cloth in which it was being cooked.

By January, the cabins finally arrived — but it was not much of a step up, consisting of just two bedrooms and a combined living room-kitchen complete with fuel stove. The bathroom, with its tin bath, could be entered only from outside the house. Water was not connected and had to be hauled by bucket and heated in the laundry copper. Nor was there any electricity, lighting being provided by Aladdin lamp and a hurricane lantern. There was a battery-powered wireless, but the Clarkes switched it only for the evening news bulletin so they could keep up with the war. When it ran down, the battery had to be taken to the motor garage in Woolbrook for recharging. With no telephone and no car, contact with family and friends was maintained through the post. If there was a family emergency, the Clarkes could be reached by telegram, the message being delivered by fettlers as they came up the line. Meat and bread came twice-weekly on the train from Tamworth, and was thrown out at the signal box; quite often the wrapping would burst, and the flies would immediately descend on the meat.

The railway department once a month issued the Clarkes a Market Pass which entitled them to travel by train to Tamworth to do their shopping. This monthly outing was the highlight of their time at Warrungen; Jean preserved carrots and beans and whatever fruit she could find in the stores. The soil was poor but a few crops survived; every bit of waste water went on that garden.

Dick, as a married man, was paid five pounds a week. Trapping rabbits became a handy way of making an extra few bob for both railway men based at Warrungen; in fact there were times when he made almost as much money catching rabbits as working for the railways — with most of the young local men away at the war and farm labour scarce, the rabbit population thrived. When it came time for the two weeks annual leave to be taken, the men would be issued with Train Passes that allowed them to go wherever NSW Government Railways provided passenger services.

In 1944 NSWGR decided to close the Warrungen loop, and Dick and Jean were moved to Casino. But rented accommodation was scarce with the war on and the town's population having swelled. Dick found his wages would not cover a rented house (and there was no rabbit trapping in Casino to supplement the wages) so they ended up boarding. However, he decided to take matters into his own hands — not something that many railway staff had the nerve to do in those days. He wrote about his accommodation problems to the Chief Traffic Manager, the result of which was a telegram telling him that there was a house at the wayside station of Banyabba if the Clarkes wanted to move there. Even though the hours were long, the work was not all that arduous. But for signalmen who manned busy stations, it was a different matter. Mount Gambier station yard in South Australia had a signal box with forty levers — red ones for signals, black for switches (changing points), and blue ones that locked the switches. As 'Johnny', a self-described old South Australian Railways shunter, describes it on his website of recollections

> ... pulling these levers during an eight hour shift was a back-breaking job and very busy with two or three engines shunting at once. The buttons above the black and blue levers are the Push buttons that had to be pressed and held in before operating any of the switch levers. If there was a train on the circuit anywhere, there was no way the cabin operator could operate the switches — everything was interlocked. The button was pushed or held in, then the switches had to be set, and then locked before a signal could be pulled 'off' to allow a train or engine to exit or be admitted to the yard or station. All this for safety reasons. So the signalman had to know in exactly what sequence the cabin levers had to be placed before any train movements could begin.

And, on top of all that, the signalman had to be fully conversant with regulations governing all the electric staff and train order safe working system — for both the South Australian and Victorian sections that applied at Mount Gambier.

Peterborough in the railway age — every road is occupied by wagons, and the platform track has a locomotive running light, perhaps on shunting duties. And this was when the South Australian station was totally narrow gauge. Later broad and standard gauges would be added, making it one of two triple gauge stations in Australia. John Mannion Collection.

Labouring in the goods yard

Lloyd Holmes had left Victorian Railways, where he had been a train examiner, to try his hand at farming in southern New South Wales. Due to allergies caused by grasses and grain dust affecting the amount of work he could on his land, he was forced to seek some extra money. Holmes ended up working as a labourer in the Albury marshalling yards in 1960, when it was still the site of the break-of-gauge between the broad (Victorian) and standard (New South Wales) gauge railways. Shift work enabled him to have time for milking and other tasks on his farm.

Holmes was one of 360 casual labourers employed by the New South Wales Government Railways Traffic Branch seven days a week at Albury, working in two shifts, and described in his book, *A Railway Life*. Working in teams of six or seven men, theirs would be the task of manhandling every item from the wagons of one railway into those of the other. Apart from parcels, mailbags and luggage, the labourers would shift

> … cartons of strawberries, cut flowers, racing pigeons in crated cages, dogs and cats, canaries, agricultural machinery parts, smallgoods, bicycles and motor bikes, skis, bundles of the farming paper *The Weekly Times,* reptiles, coffins, the odd goat in a crate — all and sundry were transhipped and sent on their way. About every six weeks, 'the Bullion' would arrive from Melbourne Mint bound for Canberra; and a gang would transfer the many small tin trunks across from the Albury Express into a special van marshalled just ahead of No. 4's [the Sydney Express) brake van. Six or seven Treasury officials accompanied the consignments of coin, being well-armed and watchful as the transfer took place. The trunks

were loaded one-high across the floor of the EHO van and these guards had mattresses, which they then laid on top for their cold and uncomfortable trip to Canberra. After the bullion transfer was completed, it was traditional that each handler and wheeler was flicked a brand new five shilling piece as a bonus from the Treasury boys.

The freight yard work raised a sweat. An LLV louvre van held 1,017 cases of bananas each weighing thirty-four kilograms, stacked to the roof. Other wagons might contain carpets, potatoes, refrigerators or other electrical appliances, onions, furniture, clothing and footwear in cartons, confectionery, hardware, pharmacy supplies, crates of new bottles, which were all shifted by the yard labourers. When Ford introduced the Falcon to Australian drivers in 1961, Albury yard workers had to become adept at driving those cars off the wagons of Victorian Railways trains and then on to standard gauge EHO wagons — and load them in reverse gear, the cars having to face the rear of the trains in order to avoid windscreen damage while in transit. Then there were the NSW wagons to be loaded with butter when the consignment arrived from Victoria; these wagons had to be filled with ice through an opening in their roofs.

There were also gantry cranes to move the heavy freight such as agricultural machinery, poles, motor vehicles, boilers and rails. Those on the evening shift broke off their work at the goods wagons to get ready for the 9.15 pm arrival of the Albury Express from Melbourne with, as Lloyd Holmes recalls, its 'mountains of mailbags, luggage and parcels'. His extensive knowledge of NSW geography meant Lloyd was assigned to the express's brake van on its arrival from Melbourne where his task was to direct the parcels, mail, newspapers and other items to the correct position to the waiting MHO van sitting on the NSW standard gauge track so that each item would be in their correct place (left or right side, near the top or way down in the pile) to be the next on hand when the train reached the station at which it was to be unloaded. He had to be a quick thinker as the destination names flashed by him — "Gulargambone, Quandialla, Grong Grong, Humula, Wait-a-While, Bukalong, Willie Ploma, Garema, Merriwagga, Urangeline East" and many others. There was no room for error as the train would stop for barely a minute at many of those places. It was further complicated by the need to know, for destinations not on the express's route, what trains connected at various junctions: this meant that, depending on the day of the week, a parcel for a particular Riverina town might be unloaded at either Junee or Cootamundra for its connecting train.

None of those wayside stations so familiar to Lloyd Holmes remains today.

Fettlers

All the railway systems across Australia had fettlers, thousands of them. These were the men who were responsible for a given length of rail — they are also known as lengthsmen for this reason — and their lives were spent travelling along that section making sure it was in good condition, and fixing anything that was wrong. It was not much of a job. You worked hard — real hard — in all weathers, lived in tents either permanently or when you were away from home; often your water had to be delivered by train.

The West Australian Government Railways' working time-table of 1953 for the Laverton and Leonora branches instructed staff that 'water for Permanent Way Gangs, must as far as possible, be supplied on Down journey' (that is, on the trip outward from Kalgoorlie, not on the return journey) and that Train 191, which ran two days a week, 'may stop at 402-Mile Post ... to set down provisions'.

The list of equipment used by a typical fettler gang testified to the backbreaking work involved. They would either carry with them or have in their huts rail tongs, spiking hammers, picks, shovels, crowbars, ballast forks, hand augers (a tool for boring holes in wood or in soil), dog-spike lifters, rail jacks and long-handled spanners.

Cec Townsley, who took a job as a fettler on the Injune branch in Queensland after coming back to Australia from service in the 1939-45 war, did not last all that long: as Cec puts it, after the army years of living tents in the middle of nowhere, he did not feel like doing the same thing for Queensland Railways, and threw in the railway work in favour of a job based in Roma. His experience would have been typical. In very hot weather, the gang of six men of which Cec was part would pitch their tent out on the job. Otherwise, they slept in a goods shed which had been built with walls of galvanised tin (no wonder they slept out in tents during hot weather) although the ganger, the man in charge, did have a house at one of the stations along the line. The first job each morning was to 'run the line' of that section for which they had responsibility to check for any problems. Otherwise, most of the time was spent lifting and packing sleepers or replacing any which were beyond their useful life. The worst part of the job was working Saturdays as well which meant that — because there was no train — anyone without their own transport was stranded in the camp for the weekend.

There were not too many trains on the Injune branch, traffic varying over the years from three a week up to nine. But that was still fewer than two trains even over a six-day week, yet such a lightly used branch required considerable manpower. It was, at 100.6 km, on the longer side as far as Queensland branches were concerned but there was not a great deal of difficult country even though there were fifty-three bridges, most of them small. Yet in 1932 five gangs of fettlers were stationed along the branch, one each based at Minka, Orallo and Injune, with two others based at two of the small sidings.

Every fettler, to a greater or lesser extent, knew how vulnerable they were on their small trolleys if they came around a curve and found themselves face-to face with an oncoming train. There were no walkie-talkies in those days; many country stations were not connected to the telephone system. While a ganger might know the timing of the daily mixed, a livestock or wheat special could catch them by surprise — an especially risky situation if the encounter occurred in a tunnel.

When they were not replacing sleepers, the fettlers — if they were located in one of the parts of Australia with lush vegetation — would regularly chip the weeds along the permanent way with a shovel, or they might have a can slung their back containing weed killer and a spray gun. The gang would also have beaters, a doubled-up piece of canvas attached to a pole, used to control burn offs of long grass alongside the railway line. They could turn their hands also to farm work when local property owners needed help — they could do such tasks as sewing wheat bags or work as roustabouts in the shearing sheds. No doubt the money helped, but for the farmers it was a solution to a labour problem at the times of the year when everyone on the land needed to find more pairs of hands.

There were many who spent who spent their working lives as fettlers; others were blow-ins — men looking to make a few quid before moving on elsewhere, or taking the job because it was the only one on offer. Or on their way to something better. Long before he entered politics and made his way to the prime ministership, William Morris (Billy) Hughes worked as a fettler in

Queensland (among other jobs, like stockman, bookseller, ship's cook, until he was taken on by the Australian Workers' Union). Edward Mabo, of the famed 1992 Native Titles case that transformed Aboriginal land ownership rights, was one, as was the writer and poet Roland Robinson after arriving as an immigrant in 1921. The Australian writer Xavier Herbert (his real name was Alfred Jackson) worked on the narrow gauge North Australia Railway, being based at Rum Jungle south of Darwin. Herbert used his experiences on the railway — and Rum Jungle — in the 1920s for his portrayal of the town of Black Adder Creek in his classic *Capricornia*. In that book, he describes train day (in those days, it ran once every two weeks):

> Train day was special to the people living on the railway, particularly to the fettlers, to whom the train brought not only mail and stores and news from civilisation in the form of gossip, but wages for the past fortnight's work and liquor for the next fortnight's drinking.

The luckier ones were stationed in towns, but many lived with their families at remote wayside stops, and then they often camped out when away on overnight trips. Lloyd Holmes recalled when, on a 1955 journey from Albury to Culcairn in New South Wales, he spotted from the carriage window at Table Top station a scene that stayed in his mind. There, besides the goods shed, sat a fettler's wife sitting outside the family's white calico tent peddling on her sewing machine.

> Somehow this unlikely domestic scene typified the spirit of the then New South Wales Government Railways: here she was, no electricity, no running water, no amenities to soften life, no protection from the heat and cold but a thin layer

of canvas, kids probably temporarily enrolled in the nearby school, and she was sewing away merrily for her family.

Or the fettler and his family might be comfortable on location if given railway department houses. However, Norman Sibraa was not one of these when he was posted to Jerilderie in the NSW Riverina in the late 1950s. As his daughter Norma Gowans remembers it, there was no railway house available in Jerilderie when the two parents with their eight children (there would soon to two more) arrived from the former posting at Yenda on the Temora-Roto line. So they set up house in the Jerilderie goods shed and Norman put in an application for a tent. When that arrived — it was a large, marquee-style tent — bags were nailed to the ground to make a floor. Norman's wife was then able to sweep up the dust that blew in and so keep the place as tidy as she expected. The children slept in the large tent, but the parents had a smaller one next to it which served as their bedroom. The family showered once a week, using water from the locomotive watering tank at the station. There was an outside lavatory and Norman from time to time would dig a new hole and move the shelter over to it. The kids would each Sunday go the local tip looking for food scraps dumped by the local greengrocer. The children's tasks during the week included carrying home food and supplies, hauled in old sugar bags, from the local shops. Norma also had the job of walking along the line on payday to pick up her father's wages from the station. During the week, their mother would walk more than half a mile to wash the family's clothes — and she did that every weekday, with Norma given the job on Saturdays. They might have lived in a tent with bags for flooring, but there were no dirty clothes left lying around. They carried the wet laundry back from the creek, and it was hung on a wire strung between two trees.

(Mind you, it was not only fettlers that endured such conditions. In the mid-1950s, the important station of Albury at the change of gauge with Victoria had, in its yards, a tent town. Here drivers, firemen, guards and their families lived in small tents with water taken from a community tap. Each staff member had six shillings a week deducted from their pay for being provided with a tent in the yard and water. How the train crews on night duty managed to sleep during the day, with all the noise of the yard, remains a mystery. But the use of tents on the New South Wales railway network lasted into the 1970s.)

Norma remembers that the locals were good to the family: when there was a local ball or other function, left-over food would be delivered to the tent. The only pullovers they had during the cold Riverina winters were the ones that formed part of their school uniforms, and they had to take these off as soon as arriving home so that the jumpers would last as long as possible. Norma said this has given her a lifetime ability to cope with the cold. (She also says her own children can scarcely believe her accounts of childhood on the railway just forty-five years ago, so different has life become.) Eventually, the family moved to Finlay and was able to acquire a railway house, which they later bought.

At least Norma and her siblings had a school to go to. Not so in August 1939 at Menindee on the line to Broken Hill. A reporter from Sydney's *Daily Telegraph* filed this report from the settlement:

> Living along the railway line between Menindee and Ivanhoe are thirty children of school age without any educational facilities. They are mostly children of railway workers. Most of them cannot read or write. On Saturday I interviewed many of the children and their parents. In seven shacks which I visited I saw no reading matter but popular periodicals.

One mother of six children said: 'I don't know enough about learning to take correspondence with the children. Anyhow, what with floods and dust storms and looking after the children I don't know I get enough time. Nearly all the children here are suffering from sandy blight [trachoma] and malnutrition'. At one siding, Kaleentha, there are seventeen children of school age who haven't had a school lesson since they came to the area.

Being a fettler meant keeping the line open. Occasionally there was variation, such as changing a set of points at one of the stations, but otherwise —day in, day out — the job of the fettler was to change sleepers under the rails. When a line had two wheat trains a day, each hauling between thirty or forty heavily laden wagons, the track took a hammering. The fettler crew usually comprised eight men who would ride out each day on their rail trike with its petrol motor (in later years the gang was provided with a truck, comparative luxury, and they no longer had to melt the frost on the rails in the winter to make it possible for the trike to gain traction). There was no shade along sections of line; it was searing heat in the summer, freezing cold in the depth of winter. You had to be fit: which is why in the post-war years applicants were given the same sort of physical tests that the military employ to check new recruits; there was a chest x-ray and doctors looked for potential problems such as hernia or bad back. That sort of fitness was needed, as they used large tong-like instruments to pull out sleepers that needed replacing, then used a shovel to clean the sleeper trench of any debris before sliding the new one in. The hardest jobs were done by the younger men in the gang; those in their fifties simply no longer had the muscle to haul a sleeper out of its trench.

Fettlers would also check the evenness of the track level by sighting along the tops of rails and packing the ballast under low spots (which were known as 'holes in the road'). The distance between the two rails was known as 'the four feet' in New South Wales where standard gauge applied and 'the five foot' in Victoria were broad gauge ruled. Devotion to the job was high: weeds in the ballast were seen as an affront to the gang looking after that section. The man responsible for driving the spike into the sleeper, using the spike hammer, was expected to be able to complete the task with three hits — any more invited derision from the rest of the gang.

A rotameter near Broken Hill, 1927. This piece of equipment was used between 1905 and 1930 to survey the line and railway structures. The men would have consulted the curve and gradient diagrams book to check their own readings. Paddy Norton Collection.

If the sleepers needing replacement were scattered along the line, the gang could manage between fifteen and twenty a day; if the replacements were targeted for one continuous section of track, then they might manage fifty a day. For the big jobs, a large workforce would be rounded up from railway stations many miles away. More than 200 men could assemble and work along a section changing all those sleepers that a foreman had marked with chalk or paint.

The engine driver

When Ian Kauschke, an engine driver based at Port Pirie in the 1950s, was booked to work freights from Adelaide, he always knew that it would be no short task. In fact, he knew it would take twelve hours from the Mile End yard at Adelaide. Fifteen of those would be spent getting just as far as Snowtown, 145 km north of Adelaide. Three crews were assigned to the working, and long shunting operations took place at each station along the way. In those days everything went by rail: bales of wool, lengths of water pipe, six-foot sheets of roofing iron, and forty-four gallon drums among them. All were loaded and unloaded by hand. On the way south, a stop at Collinsfield usually meant filling an empty wagon with crates of eggs, an arduous task for the crew in the absence of station staff; and the train just stood there waiting while the fireman walked back to help the guard carry the crates from the goods shed and stack them in the wagon. On night time workings, at most stations the local porter had clocked off after the day shift and any goods handling would be done by the train crew.

The workings of the coal stage can be seen in this picture taken at Werris Creek, NSW, on an unknown date. This appears to be an old 32 class locomotive which went through several colour schemes: the first were painted royal blue, followed by new locomotives coming out of the workshops green, followed by some maroon ones. State Records NSW.

8

They Ran the Trains

OVER THE PAST 160 YEARS, many rail groups have existed. What follows is a selection of them.

Adelaide, Glenelg & Suburban Railway Company.

Founded: 1871

Status: Taken over by South Australian government 1899.

This company had its origins in the demands from the settlers at Glenelg, now a beach suburb of Adelaide, for a rail link with the capital. The government required it to lay tracks to the broad gauge of 5ft 3 in and operate a minimum three return train services each day. There was public opposition in Adelaide to plans to lay down track down on of the city's main thoroughfares, King William Street. When laid, the tracks there were placed flush with the street surface so as not to impede horse-drawn traffic. There were no passing loops so only one train at a time could be operating, which eliminated the need for signalling and general safe working requirements in its first year.

Glenelg became a popular seaside resort once the line was open and the growth in traffic led to the construction of a loop to allow trains to pass. But public protests to trains running down the street — it did so at the other end of the line on Jetty Road, Glenelg, too — did not abate, and were joined by complaints about soot and noise. The Glenelg company was called the 'vexing monopoly'; it was said to treat its customers badly, there were complaints about timetabled trains being cancelled on race days, and about the failure to stop at certain halts.

The finances of the company were impacted by the purchase of two extra locomotives and ten extra carriages to cope with racecourse and holiday traffic, rolling stock which at other times stood idle. There had also been a merger with the Holdfast Bay Railway Company. Eventually, directors accepted an offer from the colonial government of £120,000 for the company.

Aramac Shire Council
Opened: 2 July 1913
Status: Closed 31 December 1975

This shire council owned a 66.6 km line connected at Aramac Junction to Queensland's narrow gauge network. Queensland Government Railways supervised all track maintenance to ensure it complied with government standards even though shire workers did the actual work. The stationmasters for the Aramac terminus were appointed by the government railway but other non-train staff were employed by the council.

The shire built the line after it failed to convince the state government in Brisbane that its area deserved a branch line. A £66,500 loan was secured by the Queensland Treasury. In 1915 the tramway carried 4,079 tons of general goods, fifty-three tons

Aramac Tramway's RM28 and trailers pause at what passes for a station at Bowyer. Brian Webber

Having completed its run from Aramac to link with the Queensland Railways trains, the railmotor and trailers are turned on a fork at Barcaldine during Easter 1975. Brian Webber

of timber, 23,267 bales of wool, 265,000 sheep, 578 horses, 475 cattle, 133 dogs, 117 bicycles, 1,414 first class and 5,227 second class passengers.

By 1938 the picture was quite different: that year, as road transport grew, only 1,747 passenger tickets were sold, sheep numbers were down to 6,670. The end came with the sealing of the road from Barcaldine. The last passenger service ran on 21 December 1975.

The motive power at the start was bought —in the form of steam locomotives B12 31 and B15 308 — from Queensland Railways but in 1924 the shire had built its own locomotive, numbered A1, based on the design of the Queensland Pb15 4-6-0 class. In 1963 a second-hand Queensland railmotor, RM28, was bought to speed passenger services.

Australian National Railways
Formed: 1975
Status: Assets sold 1997; wound up 2000

Established by the Whitlam Labor government as the first step toward federalising railway operations. ANR acquired Commonwealth Railways (operations in Northern Territory, the Australian Capital Territory, South Australia and Western Australia) along with Tasmanian Government Railways and South Australian Railways (excepted metropolitan passenger services in Adelaide). Victoria refused to join, seeing the move as socialism. The Adelaide-based corporation had all three gauges under its control. It closed down all country passenger services in South Australia, standardised more track (including the Melbourne-Adelaide route), introduced double-stacking of containers and upgraded main lines. Some saw its biggest mistake in focusing entirely on interstate freight and neglecting rural branch business in South Australia. It was also hobbled by the losses of the Tasmanian network.

In 1997 its freight operation was sold to Australian Railroad Group, its passenger trains (The Ghan, Indian Pacific and Overland) to Great Southern Rail.

Commonwealth Railways

Founded: 1911

Status: Merged into Australian National Railways 1975

A typical scene from the last decade of the Northern Australia Railway. Here NSU 63 heads a mixed goods on the line south from Darwin with goods and vehicles for offloading at various stops. This locomotive was built in Birmingham, England, and was powered by a Swiss-made 712 kW engine. NSU 63 entered service in November 1956. Australian National Railways.

The Federal government got into the railway business when it took over ownership from South Australian Railways of lines that operated in the Northern Territory, the narrow gauge Darwin-Pine Creek isolated section and the Port Augusta-Oodnadatta line. The Commonwealth undertook to connect the two, the railheads then being 1,700 km apart. In the event, only extensions at each end were achieved, and the gap between the two reduced only slightly by 1929: the extension of the southern line from Oodnadatta to Alice Springs and the northern line from Pine Creek to Birdum. Then came the Great Depression and work stopped.

The Commonwealth government had more resolve when it came to connecting the east and west rail systems. Work on the Trans Australian Railway began from Port Augusta in South Australia in 1912 and, the following year, from the western end at Kalgoorlie. The two railheads met on 17 October 1917, and five days later the first passenger train pulled out of Port Augusta.

Commonwealth Railways had its head office in Melbourne but the operational staff and workshops were located in Port Augusta. Until 30 June 1975, its last day in existence, the corporation oversaw five rail operations with a total route length of 3,505 km:

Australian Capital Territory: Queanbeyan (New South Wales) to Canberra (Australian Capital Territory), 8 km standard gauge. NSW Government Railways trains ran on this section.

Central Australia Railway: Stirling North (South Australia) to Alice Springs (Northern Territory). Consisted of 350 km standard gauge and 869 km narrow gauge, with break of gauge at Marree.

North Australia Railway: Darwin to Birdum (Northern Territory). Total 511 km narrow gauge.

Whyalla line: Port Augusta to Whyalla (in South Australia). Total 75 km standard gauge. When built in 1972, it was Australia's first main route to be laid using concrete sleepers.

Trans-Australian Railway: Port Pirie (South Australia) to Kalgoorlie (Western Australia). Total 1,782 km standard gauge.

At one stage, Commonwealth Railways operated under four different time zones – Eastern, West Australian, Central and a fourth between Tarcoola and Rawlinna which was set halfway between the western and central time zones (which themselves were 1.5 hours apart).

Deniliquin and Moama Railway Company
Line opened: 4 July 1876
Status: Bought 1923 by New South Wales government.

The Victorian government line winding out from Melbourne reached Echuca on the border with New South Wales in 1864. Echuca was an important transport hub as a port for river traffic on the Murray. After opposing the plan to extend the Victorian government line across the border, the New South Wales government relented and approved a private scheme for a broad gauge railway from Moama (on the opposite, and NSW, bank of the Murray from Echuca) to Deniliquin.

The only construction challenge was the bridge across the river; the rest of the 72 km route was almost flat country, and the route had only five curves. The company bought two Beyer-Peacock 0-6-0T locomotives, with a further two added later to the fleet. It had six passenger cars and sixty-one goods wagons.

While the line from 1923 became New South Wales property, trains were thereafter operated by Victorian Railways as part of the latter's broad gauge network. There were four staffed stations: Echuca, Moama, Mathoura and Deniliquin. Victorian Railways in 1926 laid a branch line from just north of Moama to Balranald.

Midland Railway Company

Founded: 1890

Status: Purchased by the West Australian government in 1964

This company was floated in London and subsequently completed a 445 km line between Midland Junction (near Perth) to Walkaway, where it connected to an isolated section of government line from the port of Geraldton. By April 1891 the company managed to get open the first 80 km section as far as Gin Gin; a few months later trains were running from the other end, 96 km to the temporary railhead at Mingenew. Thanks to a government bond issue of £500,000, the company overcame financial challenges and the entire line was opened to traffic on 2 November 1894.

The bulk of the company's revenues over the years derived from the haulage of agricultural products, but the opening of the Murchison Goldfields brought other freight as well as an upsurge of passenger numbers. Eventually three sleeping cars were added to the fleet of sitting carriages. Then, in 1915, the government completed its near parallel line northward to Mullewa, giving the state railway its own link between Perth and Geraldton. Then as road operators sprung up and began competing for passengers the Midland company bought its own road coaches and also began road freight services.

But it remained relatively busy railway. As late as 1960 the Midland carried 265,000 tonnes of freight but it was struggling to make ends meet and in 1964 the company accepted the latest government offer to sell out. Apart from transport, the line brought other benefits to those who lived along it. The Gin Gin station was made available for local community meetings and the goods shed at Three Springs in 1909 doubled as the town's first silent movie theatre.

New South Wales Government Railways

Formed: 1855 (as Department of Railways).
Status: Passenger services still operated as a government railway. Freight services privatised.

Fortunately the New South Wales rail system in its formative years attracted a giant of a figure — John Whitton. He was appointed engineer-in-chief in 1856 and, in his thirty-four years in the post, the colony saw nearly 3,330 km of new railway lines. These included the 620 km Sydney-Albury link, completed in 1881; the lines for the far north, Bourke being reached in 1885 and Wallangarra in 1889; the completion of a bridge over the Hawkesbury River north of Sydney which allowed a direct rail connection between Sydney and Newcastle. When he retired at the age of seventy, in bad health, the government granted him an annual pension of a very modest £657.

Underlying Whitton's achievements was the fact that, from the start, he built all lines to the heavy rail standards then prevailing in the United Kingdom. Not for New South Wales the cheap, light lines adopted in other parts of Australia. Not for him, either, building some of the network to narrow gauges to save money as had been done in Victoria and South Australia; very line had to be to the standard gauge.

After the main lines were completed, his attention turned to constructing railways to the interior of the colony. By 1888 the colony's rail system was carrying fourteen million passengers a year and 3.4 million tons of freight. Between 1880 and 1889 the system was extended by an average 231 km a year. Then followed, through the 1890s and up until the First World War, an extensive branch line building program. By 1920 the state's system totalled 8,100 route kilometres. The extensions continued being laid until the Great Depression struck.

Queensland Government Railways

Established in 1863 by enabling act.
Status: Freight business privatised; passenger and suburban services operate still under government ownership.

The first sod of the 34 km line from Ipswich to the Little Liverpool Range was turned on 26 February 1864. The following year the section from Ipswich to Bigge's Camp (now Grandchester) was opened to traffic. In 1867 Toowoomba was reached. And, by 1875, Queensland's rail system extended over 405 km.

The early pattern of railway building in Queensland was typified by construction of isolated systems built out from Brisbane, Rockhampton and Townsville. In 1900, the Queensland network comprised eleven isolated sections. The main coastal route from Brisbane —all 1,680 km of it — was not completed until December 1924.

Silverton Tramway Company

Founded: 1888
Status: Ceased the Broken Hill-Cockburn service in 1970. Later provided locomotives and other services.

Based at Broken Hill, the Silverton company came into being after the government in New South Wales would not allow South Australia to build rails across the border between the two colonies to reach Broken Hill (which lies near the South Australian border and observes Adelaide rather than Sydney time). But it did allow a private company to build the 56 km link to the South Australian Railways at Cockburn under the Silverton Tramway Act 1886, which specified the gauge to be 3 ft 6 in, compatible for the South Australian narrow gauge line across the border but with provision for the track to be converted to standard gauge if so required by Sydney.

The NSW standard gauge line from Sydney reached Broken Hill in 1927 but Silverton's narrow gauge connection was allowed to remain without the conversion being required. That conversion occurred in 1970 when the Perth-Sydney transcontinental standard gauge line came into being. From that time, the Silverton company continued as a shunt operator on mine lines around Broken Hill.

Silverton also operated weekly trains on the 61.8 km narrow gauge line running north from Broken Hill owned by the Tarrawingee Flux and Tramway Company. The trains hauled limestone to be used as flux in the smelters at Broken Hill. Those smelters were moved to Port Pirie in South Australia in 1898 but the residents of Broken Hill lobbied Sydney for the retention of the line, and New South Wales gave in and bought the track for £15,000, and then spent another £36,000 upgrading it. But NSW had no narrow gauge rolling stock, so contracted Silverton to run a weekly passenger train hauled by a Y class locomotive. There were also specials for picnics and race meetings.

On the services to Cockburn, the Silverton company hauled concentrates destined for the Port Pirie smelters; on the return trip, they hooked up loads of fuel and other supplies brought up from South Australia to keep Broken Hill running (the rolling stock being interchangeable with SAR to avoid transhipment at Cockburn). An overnight service from Terowie with passenger sitting and sleeper carriages was hauled from Cockburn into Broken Hill by Silverton locomotives (the company usually hooking on goods wagons as well to make full use of locomotive hauling capacity). Over its lifetime, Silverton hauled 3.4 million passengers and 54 million tons of silver-lead-zinc concentrates.

South Australian Railways

Founded: 1856

Status: Merged into Australian National

The department came into being with the construction by the government of the 12 km broad gauge line from Adelaide to Port Adelaide. This was the first totally government-built and operated railway in the British Empire.

Perhaps SAR's most ambitious project was the Great Northern Railway from Port Augusta via Quorn and on to the Oodnadatta in the Northern Territory, a distance of 639 km, and reaching Oodnadatta in 1891. By 1917 SAR had grown almost to what would be its full extent of 5,300 km of route length.

The decision to build some of the lines to the broad gauge and others to narrow led to a proliferation of break-of-gauge stations, deadly for rail's competitiveness as road transport developed. Then the construction of the transcontinental line to Port Augusta and Port Pirie by 1937, and then to Broken Hill in 1969, brought more complications with the addition of standard gauge to the mix. And it brought that South Australian phenomenon: the triple gauge stations (at Peterborough and Gladstone).

The dominating figure in South Australian rail history is William Alfred Webb. He was appointed commissioner in 1922 when the railways in that state were facing a number of problems: the rolling stock was ageing and traffic declining. His solution was to introduce new and more powerful locomotives to replace the proliferation of small engines on the system, so allowing trains to be bigger and more economic. Large capacity wagons were also introduced and some narrow gauge lines were converted to broad gauge.

Tasmanian Government Railway

Established: 1872

Status: Absorbed into Australian National Railways 1978

The Tasmanian government's involvement in railways was not of its own choosing: it was the failure of the Launceston and Western Railway Company in 1873 that meant abandoning the policy of leaving railway building to private enterprise. Following its acquisition, the government added several branch lines and extended the former private line on to Devonport. By 1897 it was possible to travel all the way by rail between Hobart and Queenstown, albeit by a circuitous route that touched the northern coastline of the state.

TGR was a constant and often serious drain on government finances. After the Second World War, the Tasmanian railway system was in a situation where most of its motive power was either obsolete or needed substantial repairing. The department ordered thirty-two new diesel-electric locomotives from English Electric, along with diesel mechanical shunters from Drewry Car Company. But steam was still needed: eighteen new such locomotives were also ordered, eight 4-8-2 H class heavy good engines and ten 4-6-2 M class mixed traffic ones. In the immediate postwar years, TGR also took surplus locomotives from other systems; these comprised four Nfb class 2-6-0 locomotives from Commonwealth Railways (they had been built for South Australian Railways between 1890 and 1892) and six standard Garratts from Queensland. The Western Express between Launceston and Wynyard was converted to diesel railcars to free up more locomotives.

The system survived, although one cannot say it ever prospered. When the Whitlam federal government (1972-75) made an offer to all states to assume control of their railways, Tasmanian politicians could not believe their luck and promptly handed over the money-eating railway system.

Victorian Railways

The Victorian Railway Department came into existence on 19 March 1856 after the colony's government had been forced to rescue the Melbourne, Mount Alexander and Murray River Railway Company (see below). In 1997 it was split into V-Line passenger and freight arms, the latter being sold to a private owner. Suburban services were sold to private companies.

After acquiring the failed private company in 1856, the department called for tenders for a railway to be built to Echuca on the Murray River and for a separate line to Ballarat. Echuca was reached in 1864, and the purchase in 1862 of the privately built line to Geelong gave Victorian Railways a route to Ballarat via Geelong, the direct line through Bacchus Marsh not being completed until 1889. Wodonga, across the river from Albury and the railhead of the New South Wales system, was reached in 1873.

The gold boom of the 1850s had been the first real trigger for rail construction in Victoria. The expansion phase lasted until the 1930s. By 1892 the network stretched over 4,666 km. In the early years of the twentieth century, Victoria had a higher route mileage than the geographically much bigger New South Wales. By 1933, Victoria's railways extended over 7,585 route kilometres.

Western Australian Government Railways

Founded: Preceded from 1877 by the Department of Works and Railways, the WAGR being established in 1890.
Status: The name finally disappeared in 2003, its freight privatised and long distance services are now operated by TransWA.

The X class locomotive, introduced in 1954, once made up a large proportion of the Western Australian diesel-electric fleet and at one stage hauled all the state's long-distance passenger trains. Here X 1007 shunts at Perth. Brian Webber.

The colony's government in Perth completed its first railway line in 1879, from the port of Geraldton to Northampton where copper was being mined. Then in 1881 the line from the other port, Fremantle, started weaving inland.

The government had decided that no farmer should be farther than fifteen miles from a railway. The result? In a period of twenty years, track mileage more than doubled with 3,200 km of lines being laid by the Railway Construction Branch, Between 1894 and 1899 more than 1,000 miles of railway lines were opened to traffic. And the building kept going: the line to Bonnie Rock was opened in 1931, to Pingrup in 1923, Newdegate in 1926 and the far inland mining town of Wiluna in 1932.

Between 1890 and 1949 WAGR also operated the Perth tramway system as well as electricity and ferry services.

OTHER HISTORIC COMPANIES

Chillagoe Railway and Mines Limited. Enabling act passed 1898, lines taken over by Queensland government 1919. This company, founded by a mining syndicate to service their mines, laid a total of 446.7 km of track from the government railhead of Mareeba, all built to Queensland Railways standards so that the then dominant government locomotive, the B15 4-6-0, could run on the lines. The company did build some of its own locomotives but wagons were interchangeable with the government system.

Commonwealth Oil Corporation. Operated between 1907 and 1932. The company's 51.6 km line ran from Newnes Junction on NSW's Great Western line to Newnes itself. Founded by London publisher Sir George Newnes who became engaged in mining shale oil to make benzene for the growing number of motor cars.

The railway was built to transport the oil and passengers. Put out of business by cheap kerosene imports.

Emu Bay Railway Company. Formed in 1897 by Tasmanian businessmen to acquire an existing mine railway. It ran 141 km from the port of Burnie on Tasmania's north coast to the mining town of Zeehan where it connected with an isolated section of Tasmanian government railway. It was absorbed in 1998 by the Australian Transport Network, then private operator of the former government railway system on the island state.

Geelong and Melbourne Railway Company. In 1853 this company starting building a railway from Geelong to Melbourne with the first train running on 25 June 1857 — but only as far as the mouth of the Yarra River, the remainder of the journey to Melbourne being made by ferry. However, by 1859 a bridge had been completed and company trains were able to run to Spencer Street station in Melbourne. It was not an economic proposition and the government acquired the company.

Great Southern Railway. This company built the 389 km rail line from Beverley, east of Perth, to the Western Australian colony's then main deepwater port of Albany, the first train running in 1889 and replacing what had been a five-day trip by road coach. The government ceded the company 12,000 acres of land for every mile of line constructed; but not enough people could be found to lease all this land, so the company ran out of funds and the railway ended up in government hands. (Incidentally, while the company provided comfortable bogie carriages these were missing one vital facility — lavatories.)

Hunter River Railway Company. Existed 1853-1855. Started building the Great Northern Railway in NSW from Newcastle to Maitland. Taken over by colony's government due to financial problems.

Kerang and Koondrook Tramway. The Swan Hill Shire Council (later renamed Kerang) built this 21.7 km line in 1889 as a means of ensuring that the river port of Koondrook received a share of goods coming off Murray River boats for transhipment to Melbourne. It was a designated common carrier with Victorian Railways rolling stock using the line from the department's terminus at Kerang. The line's northern terminus was on the main street of Koondrook. In the 1930s when a rail historian recorded details, the operation comprised a manager and twelve staff including drivers, firemen, gangers, a guard, an engineer and clerical staff. The one carriage contained a small ticket office — you bought your ticket once aboard. A return journey cost four shillings.

The line was taken over by Victorian Railways in 1952 and closed in 1983.

Launceston and Western Railway Company. Established 1865, taken over by government in 1873 after going bankrupt. This company build Tasmania's first railway, the 72.5 km broad gauge route between Launceston and Deloraine.

Melbourne and Essendon Railway Company. The line from Spencer Street to Essendon Junction (later North Melbourne) was opened on 21 October 1860. A branch was later built to Flemington race course. Locomotives and rolling stock were hired from the government but the services ceased in 1864 due to financial problems. The lines remained unused until 1872; the track had been acquired by the government in 1867.

Melbourne and Hobson's Bay Railway Company. In 1854 this company opened a short railway from Flinders Street in Melbourne to what is now Port Melbourne (when extended in 1916 to Station Pier, the line was just 4 km long). A branch line to St Kilda, a distance of 5.6 km, was opened in 1857. The company in 1865 absorbed the St Kilda and Brighton Railway Company which was going to extend the St Kilda line to Brighton, which opened in 1859, and to Brighton Beach in 1861. The entire enterprise was taken over by the Victorian government in 1878.

Melbourne, Mount Alexander & Murray River Railway Company. The purpose of the company was to build a line from Melbourne to the Murray River at Echuca, a distance of 342 km and at an estimated cost of £7.72 million. It soon struck financial problems after turning the first sod at Williamstown on 12 June 1854 and was taken over by the government in 1856.

Mount Lyell Mining & Railway Company. Established 1893, line closed in 1963 due to high maintenance costs. The 27 km line opened in 1899 to haul copper to Macquarie Harbour on Tasmania's west coast, and return with coal and supplies for the miners. It incorporated a rack system over 5 km of grades of 1 in 20 and 1 in 16.

New Redhead Estate & Coal Mining Company. 1892-1991. A 15.5 km line built to service three collieries near Newcastle, NSW. Operated by NSW rolling stock. In passenger timetables was called the Belmont branch. Passenger services ceased in 1971.

South Maitland Railway. Founded in 1918 to take over running colliery lines in the Hunter Valley, NSW. Lines were primarily used for hauling coal but the company also operated passenger and general freight trains. The first great disruption came in 1929-30 when strikes hit the coalfields and the rail services and motor bus operators began offering road services through the coalfields areas. Much of the passenger traffic returned after the strike but in 1940 the company struggled to cope with upsurge of traffic due to the war as it had been forced to sell off locomotives during the Great Depression.

Sydney Railway Company. Founded 1849, taken over by NSW government in 1855; the act passed allowing this in December 1854 was the first railway nationalisation in the British Empire. The company was established to build a railway from Sydney to Goulburn. The gold discovery at Bathurst in 1851 saw many labourers desert their jobs and the government brought 500 navvies from Britain to plug the gap. The estimated cost of the line in 1849 was £2,348 a mile; by the time the government took over, costs had ballooned to £40,000 a mile.

Tasmanian Main Line Railway Company. Founded 1871, taken over by government in 1890. The company was founded to build a narrow gauge line between Hobart and Launceston, the government requiring it to lay a third rail on the existing 18 km broad gauge line from Western Junction into Launceston. The company operated trains from 1876, with the full journey including intermediate stops taking five and a quarter hours. Over the years the government laid several branches off the TMLR line and in 1890 acquired the main line from the company.

9

Trains for all Occasions

IN THE BEGINNING, THERE was the Intercolonial Express which ran from Melbourne to Adelaide, later known as the Melbourne Express or Adelaide Express. Passenger services between the two cities started in 1887. Even the Intercolonial was a trendsetter, being the only interstate passenger train that did not involve a change of trains at a border because of changes of gauge: there was a broad gauge track running between the two colonial capitals.

In 1917, the building of the great railway project across the Nullarbor Plain opened the way for the introduction by Commonwealth Railways of the Trans-Australian between Port Augusta and Kalgoorlie, a distance of 1,689 km. From 1937, the train's run was extended to Port Pirie. Unfortunately, its connecting services were not blessed with a common gauge. In the west, a narrow gauge train from Perth met the Trans-Australian at Kalgoorlie. At the other end in South Australia, passengers boarded a broad gauge train at Adelaide for the trip as far as Terowie, then transferred to a narrow gauge service via Quorn to Port Augusta, with a further transfer to the standard gauge transcontinental train.

The Ghan first ran as a narrow gauge train in 1926 to Oodnadatta. From 1929 until 1957, it ran between Port Augusta and Alice Springs via Marree and Oodnadatta. Thereafter (until replaced by a new train on a new line) The Ghan ran as a broad gauge train to Port Pirie, then a standard gauge train to Marree and, finally, late at night, the passengers transferred to a narrow gauge train for the remainder of the journey to Alice Springs. The Ghan gained its name from the Afghan camel drivers who ran teams to carry wool and supplies to and from the rail stations along the route. In its narrow gauge days, the Ghan was notorious for being late. The first trip through to Alice Springs pulled in five hours late, but that was nothing compared to some of the delays. One driver, Bert Twilley, recalled when interviewed by the author during the last trip on the old line that, on one occasion when he was on the footplate, that journey lasted two weeks, the train having become stranded between two flooded rivers. Trips lasting a month were not unknown on The Ghan. Rivers, often dry beds for much of the year, could rise from nothing after rain and wash away bridges or even the track (which had been laid on top of the ground often without any proper formation work in order to save money). There was not much comfort to be had in the early days when with 'Short Tom' passenger cars attached. These were bogie carriages with interior seating along each wall so that the passengers faced each other. There was a centre toilet and passengers could step out into the fresh air on end platforms.

The new standard gauge Ghan is a world away, a sleek modern, air-conditoned train that seals off its passengers from the hostile environment through which it passes on smooth standard gauge tracks held in place by concrete sleepers.

Another prestige train of post-war Australia was the Brisbane Limited. It was introduced in 1952 for the 987 km Sydney-Brisbane run. The Limited, after leaving Brisbane, stopped only at Bromelton, Casino, South Grafton, Broadmeadow, Hornsby and Strathfield before easing into Sydney Terminal.

Then, in 1970, with the standardisation of the transcontinental line, came the Indian Pacific. This service now runs between Perth and Sydney via Adelaide and Broken Hill (a distance of 3,961 km) as a part of Great Southern Railways, a private passenger operator. It has first class roomette and twinette cars, with these passengers eating in the Queen Adelaide dining car. Travellers booking economy sleeping accommodation or sitting cars use the Matilda restaurant car.

Melbourne-Sydney had its share of prestige trains, none more famous than the Spirit of Progress. From 23 November 1937, this train ran on the broad gauge section of the Melbourne-Sydney route between the southern capital and Albury. It set a new standard of train luxury, and included an observation car with armchairs. The train, built at Newport workshops, had Australian timber interiors, while the shells of the carriages were made from steel alloy and streamlined. Victorian Railways assigned to the train its powerful S-class locomotives, which had a winged VR emblem painted on their noses. The engines were named after early figures in the state's history: Matthew Flinders, Sir Thomas Mitchell, Edward Henty and C. J. La Trobe. The all-blue cars owned by Victorian Railways were remounted on standard gauge bogies when the New South Wales gauge was extended into Melbourne. The train offered first class sleepers and first and economy class seating.

The Intercapital Daylight was added to this run in 1956 brought into service by Victorian Railways after it was realised a demand existed for daytime travel between the two state capitals in preference to overnight journeys on the Spirit of Progress.

An entirely new glamour train began operating between the two state capitals from 16 April 1962, the Southern Aurora. During its life, it was the most prestigious of the Sydney-Melbourne trains. Its accommodation was entirely first class sleepers, with both a lounge and a dining car. The rolling stock was built by Commonwealth Engineering and was jointly financed by what were then the New South Wales Government Railways and Victorian Railways. From 4 August 1986, the Spirit of Progress was combined with the Southern Aurora to form the Sydney and Melbourne Expresses. This latter service was replaced in 1993 by XPT operations.

There was a short-lived but brave attempt to bring some European-style elegance to Australian rail travel with the unveiling in February 1988 of the Southern Cross Express running between Sydney and Melbourne. The train included two old dining cars, which had been restored with polished timbers and brass-work. Wine was served in crystal glasses and the tableware was Wedgwood. The owner company failed in less than a year and the train was withdrawn.

NSW Express and Mail trains

New South Wales had a vast array of country trains, many of which had official names. Then there were those with unofficial names, but names that stuck and came into widespread use. Many of these were relatively recent inventions, such as the Canberra-Monaro Express which came into existence in 1955. It had replaced the Federal City Express connecting Sydney with the federal capital at Canberra and then ran on to Cooma, a total distance of 432 km. The Federal City had been introduced in 1936 as a daylight service in addition to existing night mail expresses between the two cities. The Canberra-Monaro replacement was equipped with DEB rail-cars from the beginning, whereas the superseded Federal City had been a locomotive-hauled carriage train. The DEB cars offered first and second class seating, along with meal tray and liquor service. Hostesses also regularly passed through the train with trays containing cigarettes, sweets, ice cream and nuts. The Canberra-Monaro service was withdrawn from 26 November 1988.

Other trains that carried the 'express' status were the Central West Express (in the 1940s it operated on alternate days to Parkes and Dubbo before being cut back to Orange in the 1950s) and the Far West Express (Dubbo which ran alternately to Bourke or Cobar). Additionally, there was the North Coast Daylight Express which hauled passengers the 696 km between Sydney and South Grafton. The South Coast Daylight Express ran the relatively short 153 km from Sydney to Bomaderry which was chosen as the terminus to avoid the cost of building a bridge across the Shoalhaven River to the now city of Nowra. Another short-distance but popular service out of Sydney was the Southern Highlands Express, which covered the 222 km to and from Goulburn.

Quite a few trains were split up mid-route. The Northern Tablelands Express from Sydney divided into two trains at Werris Creek, one half going to Moree, the other to Tenterfield. The Riverina Express split at Junee for Albury and Griffith via Narrandera. Just as with the daytime expresses, the Mail trains also sometimes split en route: the North Mail, for example, as with the Northern Tablelands Express, split at Werris Creek for sections to go on to Moree and Tenterfield; the South Mail replicated the division of the Riverina Express.

There was the Western Mail running to Dubbo from Sydney (formed from the merger in 1973 of the Forbes Mail and the

Dubbo Mail). There was also, at one time, overnight services bearing the titles Albury Mail, the Southern and Western Mail which began in 1879 (and which split at Parramatta, one section running to Goulburn, the other to Mt Victoria), the Temora Mail, the Bourke Mail and the Cowra Mail. There was also the Coonamble Mail which was a Saturday night service for carrying the newspapers into the countryside: it left Sydney at 11.08pm and did not reach Dubbo until 11.31am the next day.

The Mail trains, while having sleeping cars, were not much fun for those passengers who occupied the sitting carriages. One rail writer, A. R. Astle, recorded a trip to Dubbo in the 1950s during his university holidays:

> You soon lost the romantic feeling of being on a steam-hauled night train when you were crowded into an often noisy, eight-passenger compartment on a painfully slow, dirty and sometimes freezing trip. I seem to remember that the RRR (railway refreshment room) was open at Orange and you could get at least hot tea or coffee to combat your numbness in the tableland's winter. After Orange, things started to look up — you were on the home stretch; if you were on the later Bourke Mail ... the sun would be up as you approached Wellington ... Going back to Sydney was always a painful business and I usually softened the blow somewhat by missing Monday's lectures and travelling on the 'day train' where I could travel in comfort.

The Fish
Sydney-Mount Victoria
Route distance: 125 km
Status: Still operating

This was a train service started in 1881 connecting Sydney with the settlements of the Blue Mountains. It is assumed it acquired its name (first unofficial, then eventually recorded in the timetable as such) from one of its drivers, John Heron, whose nickname was 'the big fish'. He was a large, burly man in charge of engine No. 15 and the nickname soon became the unofficial title of his train — and stuck long after his death. (Heron was promoted from driving and became Inspector of Steam Sheds.) There was also a regular guard in the train's early days named Charley Pike, a factor which may have given some reinforcement to the title. While it was first just a local name, New South Wales Government Railways did eventually adopt it and even had a headboard attached to the front proclaiming it as 'The Fish'. In the 1950s, the train was described as having a club-like atmosphere where 'regular' seats were closely guarded. In later years, its afternoon service from Sydney was followed two minutes later by a Sydney-Springwood service which soon, and inevitably, earned the name 'The Chips'. There was also the daily Sydney-Emu Plains service that was known to locals as 'The Heron', although that name never made it into the official timetable.

The Camden tram

Possibly the most unusual local service was the Camden 'tram' in southwest Sydney. The line from the main line junction at Campbelltown to Camden opened in March 1882 but it was operated by the Tramways Branch of the NSW Government Railways. It was built to tramway, not heavy rail, standards; the difficult contour of the land made for some very steep grades, up to 1 in 18, so it was cheaper to follow tramway requirements. It was reclassified as a railway in 1901 but the original name stuck. The hardest part of the line was Kenny Hill. Because the line was so steep, trains often consisted of one carriage only behind a 20 class 2-6-4 locomotive. Some workings would include coal or milk wagons in addition to the passenger car (or cars), and a load of just eighty-five tons would require a second locomotive. As one article about the tram written in 1963 noted, 'The sight of two engines hauling three or four goods trucks and one or two carriages, labouring up the steep grades, was something to be seen and remembered'. After a Franciscan monastery was opened on the slopes of Kenny Hill, special eight-car trains were run on Good Fridays for the Via Cruces ceremony. These workings required not only two 20 class engines hauling the set but a third pushing from behind. The line closed on 31 December 1962, but its appeal had been lost for enthusiasts in its final years once diesel locomotives were assigned to trains on the Camden 'tram'.

Silver City Comet
Parkes-Broken Hill
Route distance: 679 km
Status: Withdrawn 1989

This was the first completely air-conditioned diesel set to run on Australian rails, the motive power provided by two Harland and Wolf diesel engines. The Silver City Comet, built in 1936, ran three days a week, providing an onward journey from Parkes for passengers travelling from Sydney on the Central West Express. At the other end, it connected at Broken Hill with the Silverton Tramway, which in turn offered a passenger service crossing the border to connect at Cockburn with South Australian Railways trains. It was also a vital link for those who lived in the more sparsely populated areas in the far west of the state. It stopped at tiny stations such as Beilpajah, Darnick and Kaleentha Loop.

The Comet itself, when introduced in 1937, was an eye-opener for rail passengers resigned normally to travelling in slow, dirty steam-hauled trains. It travelled at speeds that were much faster than steam trains but that came with a price: the combination of speed, the state of the track and the train's lightweight timber frame made for a ride with plenty of jolts. It was said no one tried to hold a cup of tea while the Silver City Comet was in motion. The introduction in 1970 of the Indian Pacific transcontinental train marginalised the Comet, but it lingered for almost two more decades.

Riding rough

New South Wales abolished third class rail travel in July 1863. The government had, when it bought the troubled Sydney Railway Company in 1855, inherited twelve third-class carriages. These were enclosed to only about half-way up each of the two sides, making for unpleasant travel in wet weather. Moreover, the compartment ceilings allowed standing height of just 5ft 6in, which meant that men could not stand up in an era of tall hats. The four-wheeler carriages had plain wooden boards for seating and could accommodate thirty-six passengers. While Sydney had abolished this class, Victorian Railways decided in 1869 to introduce third class on its trains. Initially, they attracted large numbers of people wanting to pay cheaper fares but soon there were complaints about the standard of accommodation: there were plenty of remarks about 'sheep trucks' and 'dog boxes'. Moreover, by 1870 Victorian Railways found their passenger receipts had fallen even though more people were travelling. So, initially, the effort was made to lure passengers back to second class by upholstering those seats. That had little effect in terms of luring people to pay more and so, on 31 October 1870, they were to be given no option with third class travel being abolished on Victorian Railways.

Even the dead went by rail

Trains were once part of the funeral business. There was built within Sydney Terminal yards the Gothic-style Mortuary Station. It was here that funeral parties, including the recently departed, set out for Rockwood Cemetery. The station was opened on 1 January 1869, and trains included designated hearse cars. The 1879 Railway Guide of New South Wales advised that, on trains to Haslem's Creek where the cemetery was located (it would later be called Rookwood, finally Lidcombe), corpses would be carried free of charge and the friends of the corpse could travel for one shilling a piece; however, in the case of pauper's funerals, both the corpse and grievers were to be allowed free passage. Historian Cyril Singleton recorded that, in 1902, funeral trains consisted of old-style side door carriages, but added: 'It is assumed patrons had their own worries sufficient to overlook the abominable coaching stock provided'. New South Wales was then so short of rolling stock that the afternoon funeral train, after depositing the mourners back at Mortuary Station, then was shunted into the main station to become the 5.22pm service to Homebush. However, on 20 February 1938 Mortuary Station was closed after sixty-nine years in the funeral train business. The few funeral trains required thereafter left from the main steam station at Sydney, and the former Mortuary was renamed Regent Street and thereafter used by 'dog trains' departing for greyhound race meetings at Wollongong, Dapto, Gosford and Wyong.

To the north of Sydney, Newcastle also had a station at Honeysuckle to serve funeral parties moving to the Sandgate Cemetery. A 700 metre spur line ran into what was initially called the Newcastle General Cemetery, and from 1881 funeral trains ran from Newcastle every afternoon as required. Between 1883 and 1903 a dead-end mortuary station was used for the departure of these trains, then reverting to Newcastle itself. Each Mother's Day, two trains were run to the cemetery and in 1964 two-car diesel sets were used for Sunday afternoon services for those visiting graves.

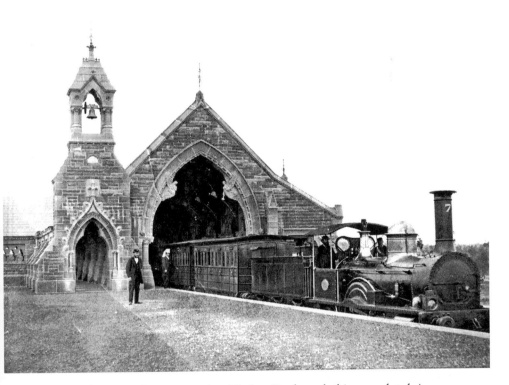

A funeral train at Cemetery station No. 1 at Rookwood, this scene dated circa 31 December 1865. Locomotive No. 7, with a 2-2-2 wheel arrangement, is coupled to two carriages in the style of Wright & Sons second class cars built in 1855. The building was demolished in the 1960s before heritage consciousness took hold. State Records NSW.

In Melbourne, there was until 10 December 1950, a 2.5 km branch track from the main Dandenong line to Springvale Cemetery. Funeral trains went down the branch, opened on February 7, 1904, and were equipped with special hearse cars. Corpses travelled free of charge, Victorian Railways covering its costs from the fares paid by the mourners. The line was electrified in 1922.

The 'Lander' Trains

In the early 1950s, Queensland Government Railways introduced new, steel passenger cars for use on its inland long-distance services. The trains were air-conditioned, and buffet cars were added to replace long refreshment stops. These trains were

The *Inlander* (Townsville-Mount Isa) 970 km.

The *Midlander* (Rockhampton-Winton) 864 km.

The *Westlander* (Brisbane-Cunnamulla, with auxiliary service to Quilpie) 971 km to Cunnamulla, 999 km to Quilpie. It split at Charleville with the two carriages detached for Quilpie being known as the 'flying flea'; today it terminates at Cunnamulla.

First class sleeping compartments, complete with Dunlopillo mattresses and lightweight rugs, were provided on all three trains; these compartments also featured a fold-out wash basin and a collapsible writing table. Second class sleeping compartments had three bunks, one above the other, and you were expected to bring your own bed linen and blankets. The three trains offered a reliable, if not all that fast, service on the three main inland arteries of the Queensland rail system. On sections laid with light rails, speed had to be reduced to 48 km/h and there were plenty of wayside stops. If you boarded the Westlander at Cunnamulla at 9.00am, you made yourself as comfortable as you knew you would not be in Brisbane until lunchtime the following day. And you would have plenty of time to inspect from your seat the tiny settlements of Nardoo, Offham and Claverton Sidings as the train stopped there, and at many other wayside stations. But the trains were introduced in an era when roads were still rudimentary, so the train services were welcomed by the locals.

The Gulflander

Normanton-Croydon
Route distance: 151 km
Status: Operating

This Queensland train is said to 'go from nowhere to nowhere' and today survives as a tourist attraction. The Gulflander's isolated section of railway is a legacy of grandiose dreams that began in the 1870s (and endure today) for a transcontinental route across northern Queensland. The decision was made to begin track construction from the port of Normanton in the direction of Cloncurry, so providing an inland route from the port for all the cattle country along its planned route. But then gold was discovered near Croydon in 1885 and that triggered a decision to built the line in that direction instead. The teams laid steel sleepers rather than wooden ones due to the presence of termites; the hollow steel filled with mud also averted the need for ballast, while the weight prevented the track moving during flooding. The track was opened to Croydon in 1891, the service being operated by steam train. Since 1930 railmotors have operated the service. There were as many as 7,000 people living at Croydon by the time the first train arrived, but the gold was worked out by the 1920s. The rail service survived into the modern era because it was the only form of transport during 'the wet'. The northern terminus, Normanton, is located 80 km upstream on the Norman River and was developed as a port for the cattle and gold industries. In the 1970s the author Patsy Adam Smith visited the Normanton-Croydon line and reported there were eight men keeping it going, four of whom were Thursday Islanders. The ganger each week took his team out on the line, and they camped variously at the sidings along the line. The line's officer-in-charge had to be qualified as a fitter, a manager and paymaster. This man also operated as stationmaster at Normanton and train driver. The railmotors of the time — the AEC and Panhard machines — needed maintenance work almost every time they returned to Normanton. In latter years, the train has achieved fame as a tourist attraction. In the mid-1970s the Queensland government considered closing the isolated railway; in 1974 it cost $63,800 to keep the service running for a return of just $3,340.

The Tasman Limited — it arrived too late

Hobart — Wynyard
Route distance: 378 km
Status: Withdrawn 28 July 1978

Starting a new long distance passenger train service in the 1950s was a considerable challenge. This was precisely the decade that saw an explosion in road transport — better buses, better roads and, increasingly, more cars in private ownership. Moreover, the route of what then became Tasmania's only named train ran parallel to bus services that actually involved less travelling time than did the train. The 378 km rail trip took almost nine hours; the time as far as Launceston was four and a half hours, compared with two hours by road. The Tasman Limited departed Hobart at 9.20 am and drifted into Wynyard at 6.05 pm. Between Ulverstone and Wynyard train speeds went as low as 30 km/h due to sharp curves and steep grades. That the train lasted as late as 1978 is astonishing given that, in its latter years, it was very poorly patronised. The Limited was introduced in 1955 as a locomotive-hauled train and by 1958 it consisted of four carriages and could accommodate 152 passengers. The Tasman Limited was an idea thirty years too late. It was certainly a comfortable way to travel, the carriages — the only articulated ones ever built in Australia — had rotating, air-cushioned reclining seats, large windows and bright curtains. Meals were delivered on trays to passengers in their seats and Tasmanian Government Railways boasted that their hostesses would even heat a baby's bottle if need be. These hostesses were known for their friendly service and were much liked by passengers. The train's disappearance caused considerable anger in the country towns it had served but, in the end, it was missed more by rail enthusiasts than the general public of Tasmania.

Railcars, railmotors and diesel sets

On other than main lines, it was often uneconomic to provide steam-hauled carriage sets — there was rarely an occasion when the number of travellers would fill such a train. Then, as road transport started to compete for passengers, the railways looked for ways to replace the then most common form of country passenger service — the mixed train (usually consisting of one or two carriages at the end of a rake of wagons) — because it was far too slow, with trains stopping to shunt at almost every wayside station. The answer, and it was a very successful answer for many decades, was the self-propelled rail vehicle — the railcar, and its variants.

Steam railcars

In the age before the modern petrol or diesel engine, steam was the only viable method of propulsion. South Australian Railways operated steam-powered railcars between 1883 and 1924. Its first venture was the importation from Belgium of a double-decked steam railcar. Steam was raised in an area on the lower deck, next to which was placed the baggage compartment. Passengers could sit there or on the upper deck. The car was first assigned to the Strathalbyn-Victor Harbor run. However, the vehicle struggled to climb the grades of up to 1 in 55 and was transferred to Adelaide in 1885, where it ran on the line owned by the Largs Bay Land and Investment Company (SAR provided all rolling stock and services on that private line). In the 1890s, the car was transferred

NJAB No. 1 steam railmotor, popularly known as the 'coffee pot'. and its passengers pose for the cameras. The file on the photo says it was taken 'somewhere between Quorn and Hawker' in South Australia. Built in 1906, it worked in service until 1935 and is now preserved. National Library of Australia.

to run between Woodville and Grange. It was scrapped in 1910. In 1906, SAR bought two narrow gauge 22-seater Kitson steam cars. One was placed on the Quorn–Port Augusta run, and was later sold to Commonwealth Railways, in 1926, for use between Port Augusta and Oodnadatta. It was renumbered NJAB No. 1. The other vehicle was assigned to the South East Division of SAR. These railmotors were intended to cut operating costs by having the steam engine and the carriage as one vehicle.

In 1923, Commonwealth Railways ordered a Sentinel-Cammell steam railcar and this entered service in October the following year. It was an all-steel car, with one-end control and a lavatory for passenger use. A vertical boiler was mounted in front of the driving cabin. The boiler had a central chute through which coal was dropped on to the fire. It had the capacity for thirteen hundredweight (about 660 kg) of fuel and three hundred gallons (1,364 litres) of water. This car operated between Darwin and Katherine until October 1936.

T. Southwell Kelly recalled a journey on the Sentinel, which soon became known as 'Leaping Lena' for the state of its riding qualities. He recorded that it pulled out of Darwin station with

... 'a series of jolts and jerks, which it maintains with unfailing regularity throughout the journey, so that one braces oneself in readiness for the next shattering jar and is disappointed if it does not occur'. He watched ahead as the narrow gauge rails 'stretched out in front through a tapering clearing; not the shining rails of the southern lines, but rust encrusted, for the trains run but once a week. The monotony of the Australian bush, mile after mile of the same type of stunted trees and scrub, is maintained to the terminus.'

Victorian Railways was, like SAR, also interested in steam railcars and by 1883 had imported a Kitson unit. This differed from other contemporaries in that its power unit could be detached from the passenger section and a replacement coupled instead. This vehicle, known as the 'Rowan Car', seated twelve passengers in first class and thirty in second. It made its test run to Bendigo and back but thereafter provided services around Melbourne, including to Box Hill and Lilydale. This car was withdrawn in 1892. Twenty years would pass before Victorian Railways again tried steam railcars, this time importing a Great Western Railways-type Kerr Stuart system. It was clearly not a great success because VR ordered no further cars, and the first was withdrawn in 1924.

In its early years, Western Australian Government Railways did go as far as having a steam railcar designed, but progress went no further. In 1932, however, WAGR committed to a standard, fifty-two seater Sentinel railcar which operated initially on a variety of country lines but from 1939 was used on suburban services between Perth and Armadale to fill the long gaps between steam train passenger services on this increasingly busy corridor line. It was notoriously difficult to fire, and WAGR staff could use only Newcastle coal as no other coals could provide heat sufficient to get the steam pressure to the required level.

Queensland Railways operated an unusual service, a tram–train in Rockhampton. This ran along a public thoroughfare between Stanley Street and Lakes Creek, a distance of eight miles. A small 4-4-0 locomotive was attached to a bogie and the vehicle stopped at all the cross streets. In 1923, the steam railcar was replaced by French-designed Purrey steam trams, the service ending when bus operations became popular in the 1930s.

The year 1931 saw Tasmanian Government Railways enter the world of the steam railcar with the purchase of two

Sentinel-Cammell vehicles, numbered SP1 and SP2, which had 100 horsepower capacity. They carried eighteen first class and twenty-two second class passengers on nightly services between Hobart and Launceston, covering the 213 km run in four and a half hours. TGR was pleased with the experience and in 1934 ordered two further cars (SP3 and SP4). These cars took over the main line runs, leaving SP1 and SP2 to be assigned to duties on the other lines. In 1937, five more cars (SP4-SP9) entered service. Parts became a problem during the second world war and operations of the steam railcars became intermittent. They were used only occasionally after the war.

The diesel era

In 1951, the Commonwealth Railways introduced the Budd RDC air-conditioned railcars which were driven by two General Motors diesel engines. The railcars were capable of speeds above 110 km/h. In fact, in a test run held on 29 April 1951, a Budd set ran from Port Augusta to Kalgoorlie. It completed the journey in nineteen hours with an average speed of 89 km/h, at that time the fastest long-distance speed in Australian rail history. The Budd actually got to 144 km/h on the famed 478 km long, straight stretch across the Nullarbor. These cars ran between Port Pirie Junction and Port Augusta, the only two towns of any size and population on the standard gauge Trans-Australian Railway. Some runs were extended to Tarcoola.

But the state systems had experimented very early in the piece with diesel cars. By 1960, more than 1,330 such railmotors or railcars were operating in the NSW system.

In 1919, New South Wales Government Railways converted a road lorry to run on rails. Called Rail Motor No. 1, it was formed from a five-ton truck with the front axle replaced by a four-wheel bogie. A new body was built to accommodate thirty-three seated passengers. It made its test run to Waterfall, on what is now the extremity of the Sydney suburban system, and ran at about 40 km/h. From 1 October, it was assigned to Lismore where a light four-wheel trailer was added containing a guard's compartment and space for seventy-two cream cans. Rail Motor No. 2, named *Kathleen,* was a converted American suburban car FA 1864, equipped with a 100 hp engine and divided into two compartments seating a total of fifty-three people. On 29 April 1921, it was assigned to run on the Barraba branch line from West Tamworth. However, after numerous failures in traffic, this car was withdrawn and returned to its original form. As a conventional passenger car, it was still working in the Newcastle district in 1967.

Rail Motor No. 3 was the first of the memorable CPH rail motors. In November 1923, CPH 3 was assigned to the Riverina where it ran three days a week on each of the Culcairn-Holbrook and Henty-Rand branch lines. The CPH railmotors carved for themselves a special place in New South Wales rail history, and several have been preserved in running order. They ran on country lines in most parts of the state, and, in 1929, were drafted to work on parts of the Sydney suburban system which had yet to be electrified, first out of Bankstown and to Cowan in the north and Waterfall in the south. For some of the cars, their last years were spent based at Wollongong before electrification came to that part of the system.

After World War II, New South Wales introduced the 600 class railcar, notable for introducing driving controls in the trailer as well as the power car (so making shunting unnecessary at journey's end) and also allowing multiple units to be lashed together for single-driver operation. These rail units were designed to run on the higher density branch lines, replacing steam-hauled

Back home. The railmotor drops off passengers at an unidentified New South Wales station, probably in the Riverina. State Rail Authority.

Part of the magnificently restored fleet of CPH railmotors at Cooma, New South Wales. Operated by the Cooma Monaro Railway, at cmrailway.org.au

carriage trains. A variation on this design was the 900 class that became identified with some of the longer-distance train services such as the Northern Tablelands Express. They were easily split which allowed the train to be cut in two at Werris Creek for runs to the two separate destinations in the north of the state, and then be joined again at the same junction on the return to Sydney.

Railmotor 905 arrives at Cooma, south of Canberra, in 1983 with the daily passenger working from Sydney. The passenger service is long gone but the scene to some extent remains as Cooma station is now the headquarters for a rail preservation group. Robin Bromby.

William Webb, the Commissioner for South Australian Railways, introduced Model 55 railcars in 1924 for use on country lines where there were insufficient passenger numbers to justify a full passenger train. The cars, made by the Brill Company, soon became known as the 'Tin Hares'. They were later switched to suburban running until withdrawn in 1968. Two years after the Tin Hares appeared, Webb brought in another railcar from the United States, Brill's Model 75. Then SAR went on to build its own version at the Islington workshops. These also operated mainly over country branches and lasted until 1971.

Another innovation, this time in the 1930s, was the introduction of the Faegol railcars, which were based on road omnibus bodies, complete with a long protruding bonnet with headlights mounted on either side over the mudcaps. These were to become familiar on the isolated system on South Australia's Eyre Peninsula, where the first line opened in 1907 and tracks reached Buckleboo by 1926. In 1915, South Australian Railways tried a small German-built motor engine on this line but it proved unsuccessful. Therefore, SAR decided to convert four Faegol motor coaches that had been used for its road passenger services to Victor Harbor, Gawler and Mannum. At Islington workshops, the buses were given a front bogie and two trailing wheels at the back. After a lavatory had been added, there was seating for twenty passengers and a trailer car was added to carry perishables, mail and parcels. From August 1931, the first of these cars took over from steam-hauled passenger trains from Cummins to Kimba, and later Buckleboo, and Cummins-Minnipa. All four were in service by May 1933, taking over from the Thevenard trains (reducing the 433 km journey time from eighteen and a half hours to twelve) and also providing a new service to Penola. Some were replaced in 1936 by bigger Model 75 railcars and two Faegols were transferred to work Naracoorte-Kingston. The last Faegol car operating on the Eyre Peninsula, with No. 109, took place on 17 August 1961.

South Australian lines were familiar territory for the Bluebird trains, built at the Islington workshops between 1955 and 1959 for South Australian Railways (and were part of the transfer of SAR to Australian National). The cars, painted blue and silver, were named after local bird species: Bluebird 101 was called 'Grebe' and 230 was 'Quail'. They operated to Victor Harbor, Mount Gambier, Peterborough and Port Pirie. In 1972, SAR adapted some of the cars to allow for a buffet section offering light meals and snacks, but by the 1980s these buffet operations had been withdrawn on all but the Mount Gambier service. The last Bluebird was decommissioned in 1993. At about the time when the Bluebirds arrived on the scene, SAR introduced a railcar version called the 'Red Hens' for working on Adelaide suburban systems.

Queensland also depended on railcars or railmotors for services on branch and country lines. The most famous was (and is) the Gulflander, as noted earlier. But, so far as the main Queensland network was concerned, the mid-50s saw the then new 1900 class railcars, the first stainless steel railcars in the Commonwealth. They were fashioned after the Budd cars, were built by Commonwealth Engineering and ran on a variety of suburban, inter-urban and branch services. The SCR-1 version could take fifty-eight passengers, while the SEC-2 held fifty people and 2.5 tons of luggage.

Among Victoria's early experiments were two McKeen railmotors, including trailers, bought from the United States in 1912. They were noteworthy for having windows shaped like portholes and for their rounded ends. Powered by a 200 hp Alecyl engine, they could theoretically make 95 km/h, but never proved satisfactory when assigned to Warrnambool-Hamilton and Ballarat-Ballan services, starting on 13 May 1912. In 1919, they were converted to ordinary carriages and assigned to the Newport-Altona line.

Queensland Government Railways imported five McKeen cars and in November 1913, the South Brisbane-Sunnybank service was taken over by these rail-motors. They also served around Ipswich. One of their shortcomings was that, because there was no guard's compartment, milk, cream and fruit were carried in the very hot engine room. They were also heavy on fuel. In 1914, QGR tried to find a better use for them by converting Nos 2 and 5 into tourist cars. These were done out with settees, lounge chairs, tables, lockers, an ice chest and a lavatory. But by 1920, the McKeen cars were rarely used.

A large fleet of railcars served Victoria's busy country passenger network in the 1950s and replaced mixed trains on most branches. From Spencer Street station in Melbourne they ran to Wangaratta, Daylesford, Wonthaggi, Bacchus Marsh, Mansfield and Heathcote. Smaller cars operated on regional routes such as Rushworth-Seymour, Ararat-Avoca-Maryborough, Cobram-Numurkah-Shepparton, Maryborough-Castlemaine, Wodonga-Tallangatta, Yarrawonga-Benalla, Pinnaroo (South Australia)-Ouyen, Horsham-Goroke and Ararat-Hamilton; these served as feeders to the main line passenger trains, enabling country people to get to Melbourne and back in a day.

Suburban trains

Australia's first railways were mostly suburban railways. The first line in Melbourne ran a short distance to Port Melbourne. In Sydney, the first line was to Parramatta. In Adelaide, a private company connected Glenelg with the city. The basis for Perth's suburban railway system was laid when, on 1 March 1881, a 32 km section opened between Fremantle via East Perth to Guildford. Then, in 1883, the line south to Pinjarra was completed, with Armadale being the limit of suburban train operations. In 1885, a small branch was laid from Bayswater to Belmont, the main purpose of which was to carry passengers travelling to and from the Belmont Racecourse. Brisbane was the notable exception. Its first line was to link Ipswich with the capital, not to connect the suburbs with the central city.

In all state capitals, services were expanded to meet the ever-increasing urban population. In all these places, too, the jungle that is their road systems ensured that the railways had a significant transport role, even though, in Sydney's case at least, it came close to buckling under the strain.

But it was not just the capital cities that had suburban rail services. Townsville had trains running out to Brookhill and Stewart's Creek (later named Stuart); eighty services a week were operating to Stuart in the 1950s. From Cairns, suburban railmotors ran to Aloomba. Maryborough and Toowoomba also had short-lived suburban services. Mildura in Victoria had a suburban service between 1922 and 1928, serving Red Cliffs south of the town and Merbein to the north using a railmotor and trailer.

Kalgoorlie claimed to be the smallest town in Australia ever to have a suburban rail service. In fact, it was argued that around 1900 the Golden Gate station in the outskirts of the mining capital was the busiest station in Australia; it was certainly seeing more train services at that time than Perth. A loop-line around Kalgoorlie served eleven stations; at Golden Gate trains would leave every ten minutes when there were shift changes at the mines, which worked three shifts around the clock. Up to sixty-one trains a day operated on the loop and the line was also used to bring equipment to the mines (boilers, crushers and winder motors) and also fuel (mainly firewood to be used to keep the mine boilers alight). This wood was supplied to Kalgoorlie on private tramways along a network at the ends of which more than 2,000 men felled trees. (See below.) Golden Gate had two stationmasters and a large staff

AEC railmotor No. 1 and trailer MT1 are seen here at Mildura station in June 1925. The number of officials posing suggests that was the inaugural run to Merbein. John Thomson Collection.

An AEC railmotor stands at Red Cliffs station after arriving at Mildura. Wilf Henty.

of porters and clerks. Boulder City station had three passenger lines, an island platform linked by overhead footbridges and a staff of twelve. Kalgoorlie's electric tram service started in 1904, and most of the passengers who had used loop-line trains switched to the new trams. However, the railway still carried freight with train services lasting until 1974.

* * *

OVER THE DECADES before motorised road transport and paved highways became ubiquitous, the railway systems were involved in the operation of specialist train services of many types. Some were for communities beyond the main cities, others were to serve the needs of the railways themselves. In the case of water trains it was to serve both; the people struck by drought on the land and the rail workers and locomotives as well. These are some of them:

Rail ambulances

Queensland Railways built ten rail ambulances during the 1920s that were based in outback towns to cope with medical emergencies. They were operated by the Queensland Ambulance Transport Board. Seriously ill people in areas remote from hospitals could often not be transported to a doctor because of the state of the roads. Before the ambulances were built, trains had been used to transport very sick or badly injured people. But these ran to schedules whereas the ambulance could be dispatched in response to a specific crisis. Local districts raised money towards the costs of the rail ambulances. One newspaper account of 1921 advised of a Sunday fund-raising excursion to a small settlement of Wyandra with tickets at six shillings for adults and three shillings for children, where the excursionists could fish, go boating or shooting.

The rail ambulances were painted white and had prominent red crosses on their sides. The roofs were made of canvas. Their operation required a qualified railways department driver to be in charge, along with one other rail staffer being on board. Charleville got its rail ambulance in 1929. On the lighter branch lines, the ambulance was limited to a speed of 24 km/h on the straight and 9.5 km/h on curves. The vehicle was very light and would easily have been derailed had it struck any object on the line. When the brakes were applied, the wheels tended to slide along the rails rather than grip them. By 1945 the Charleville ambulance base had two road vehicles, and used the rail ambulance only when the roads were made impassable by flooding or at night when visibility was poor. The rail ambulance served until 1965 and was subsequently bought by the Charleville District Historical and Cultural Society and fully restored.

Another is preserved at Mareeba; it was not conceived as a rail ambulance but, after long service in a freight role, would end up as one. It was a 45 hp AEC model 506, originally a London bus, which was converted for railway use. Between 1926 and 1940, it ran on the Milla Milla branch transporting cream for the Atherton Butter Factory with a Queensland Railways Department driver. It was then left unused for most of the war years. The Mareeba Hospital Board bought the machine after the war. The engine was rebuilt by the QR locomotive foremen at Mareeba after which it went to QR's Townsville workshops where the body was restored. In April 1949, the car was finally used as an ambulance on lines south and west of Mareeba and by 1964 had clocked a total of 55,960 km in that role. After that year, the ambulance was put into use only when roads were flooded and rail was the only means of transport. Government policy eventually turned to air transport to move sick or injured people, but this Mareeba ambulance did make the occasional foray until 1983.

In 1939, Newport workshops at Melbourne completed the first ambulance carriage (as opposed to the self-propelled Queensland models). It was built for the Defence Department, the first part of a plan for a complete hospital train of sixteen cars, including staff cars, an operating theatre, dining car and a stores car along with bed space for 360 casualties. This first ambulance car was converted from a side-door excursion Tait carriage, BPL 82, and was fitted out to accommodate forty-one patients arranged in triple tiers along the side walls. The car was painted moonstone grey with large red crosses on the roof and sides.

Children's health cars

This service originated from a scheme developed by a minister and his wife appointed to the Methodist Far West Mission, a position that brought with it a parish of some 145,000 square km of the New South Wales outback. In 1924, the Reverend Stanley Drummond and Lucy Drummond arrived in Cobar where they found many families living in dire poverty due to the closure of the mine near the town, and their children's illnesses often going untreated. This situation, however, was not unique because children in many parts of rural Australia suffered disease and illness without recourse to medical services. It was the closure of the Great Cobar copper mine in 1914, followed by other mine failures, that brought economic misery to this outback town. Its population, about 10,000 while the mines were booming, had shrivelled to 1,250 by the time the Drummonds arrived.

The result of the Drummonds' posting was the Far West Children's Health Scheme which began operation as the Great Depression was getting under way. Initially, one railway carriage was converted to be a Travelling Baby Clinic. It was staffed by a nursing sister and part of the car was converted into her living quarters: a bedroom, bathroom, kitchenette and even a refrigerating plant. The rest of the car was fitted out as a consulting room and clinic. Gauze was placed over windows to keep out flies and mosquitoes while shades protected nurse and babies from the sun. No. 1 Clinic Car, as it was designated, began service in 1931 and was sent out on the Bourke, Brewarrina and Cobar lines.

The Reverend Stanley Drummond is pictured inside one of the baby clinic cars, watching as a baby is weighed by the nursing sister while poses looking on.
Great Cobar Heritage Centre.

This photograph was taken in late 1957 at Byrock railway station (between Nyngan and Bourke in northern New South Wales). Sister Godfrey is watching from the carriage while Robin and Rose Mitchell return to their FJ Holden with baby Lynette. Great Cobar Heritage Centre.

Sister Brooks was the first nurse. She would spend between two and ten days in each locality caring for the infants brought from all over the local districts. Apart from the priority of having their babies checked and perhaps treated, the mobile clinics were a major social event for the mothers and a welcome break from the routine and drudgery of their lonely lives. In her last tour in 1934 before she returned to Britain, Brooks saw about 450 babies. Such was the success of this service that the New South Wales Government Railways agreed to convert two other cars. No. 2 Clinic Car, under Sister Kellie, operated to Walgett while No. 3 Clinic Car, under Sister McInnes, plied the railway sidings all the way to Mungindi near the Queensland border. The cars, usually attached to goods trains, would be dropped off at a siding as part of normal shunting duties with the carriage later being collected by another train to be hauled to the next wayside station.

One of these carriages has been restored and it's now on display at Cobar's heritage centre.

Farming trains

In the 1930s, Victorian Railways Commissioner Harold Clapp took his campaign to help the farmer beyond selling fresh produce at railway stations. He established the 'Better Farming Train'. The consist of fifteen vehicles was painted bright orange and the con-verted wagons or carriages offered displays on the management of both stock and crops: tobacco, pigs, dairying, beekeeping, potatoes and pasture. And the livestock displays meant carrying live animals on the train. The train toured Victoria between 1924 and 1935, spending a day at each centre. There was something, too, for the farmers' wives; they could attend lectures by nurses about infant welfare, or watch cooking or sewing demonstrations. The *Journal of Agriculture* reported that the food lectures concentrated on simple fare such as dried fruit, soups, casseroles, and how to make pastry. All these skills would have been vital on farms where there was little spare cash and the wives laboured from dawn to dusk. Like the mobile baby clinics in the Far West of New South Wales, the Better Farming Train's visit was a welcome break in the humdrum drudgery that both men and women faced on the farm. They could dress up, go to the local railway station, and probably spend as much time talking to other people from around the district as they did attending the lectures and inspecting the displays.

The centenary train

Between February and June 1941, Victorian Railways had in service the Centenary-Jubilee Train, marking the foundation of Victoria, the granting of self-government and the gold rushes. Eleven BPL cars were stripped and, with their end doors removed, formed a line of carriages through which the public could walk from one end to the other. Hauled by locomotive N430, the train carried pictures from the then National Art Gallery, models of goldfields, rare manuscripts and prints covering Victoria's early history, displays for the Air Force, Army and Navy and a display showing the planned Snowy Mountains Scheme. There was also an entertainment unit which provided shows in the towns visited. The train travelled a total of 10,040 km, stopped at 168 stations and was inspected by 548,000 Victorians.

Tea and Sugar Train

This was the name bestowed on the weekly supply train which served the railway settlements along the Trans Australian Railway. It ran weekly from Port Augusta and provided a shopping service for the railway employees and their families. The train began running in 1915, before the completion of the transcontinental link, and it carried a butcher shop and a van selling fruit and vegetables. A car with a dispensary was also provided in the consist for many years. The problem of lack of refrigeration was overcome by the cartage of live sheep which were slaughtered as and when the meat was needed. There were, in fact, two such trains until the transcontinental line was completed. One ran from Kalgoorlie to the western railhead while the other was based at Port Augusta. By 1920, and the completion of the line, one train set was equipped with purpose-built cars rather than hastily converted goods wagons, and these in turn were replaced in 1941 by even more modern rolling stock. The existence of the train meant that the railway staff along the line could buy all their provisions at reasonable prices, whereas goods would have been much more costly had they needed to be freighted at the expense of a private merchant. The train also included sitting passenger cars for the use of Commonwealth Railways employees travelling on the line. The Tea and Sugar's regular 1,048 km run entailed forty-six stops en route.

Water trains

When drought struck the Australian continent, trains played a vital role. First, they were used to evacuate stock to other regions or for slaughter. But trains also played an important role in the pre-road era of transporting water to the dry areas (and they also had to cart water to stations inland for use by steam locomotives and by their own staff scattered through remote areas of the state). NSW Government Railways initially used D and S class wagons fitted with a canvas lining for transporting water, but in 1917, they produced special tank wagons each capable of holding 29,000 litres and smaller, 22,700-litre Ka wagons that were used to supply fettlers' tanks and other rail installation. Cobar was one town that depended on water trains in times of drought until it was connected to a dependable supply in 1965 with the laying of a pipeline to the town.

Many track maintenance staff lived in camps with no assured local water supply in dry times. Every third Monday of the month, for example, a water train would travel between Nyngan and Byrock on the Bourke line in New South Wales, and these trains were also a regular feature on the Cobar line. When Broken Hill ran out of water, the tank wagons would be filled up from the Darling River at Menindee where a special siding had been laid. Allen Gordon, who was a fireman based at Dubbo in 1945, was sent on loan to Broken Hill to crew water trains to and from Menindee, which involved a round trip of 230 km. He was one of eighty railway crew seconded for the work and at that stage there were seventy-six water trains each week.

In times of drought, the railways were pressed into action to move water. Here a train discharges its load at Cobar in northern New South Wales. The water is being emptied into wood-lined trenches after which it will be loaded into water carts for delivery to local residents. Great Cobar Heritage Centre.

On the line inland from Brisbane to Charleville, steam locomotives had attached a water gin, or wagon, containing enough
water to supply their water needs over the entire and sometimes
long distances between local water supplies. This practice ended
in 1951 when a water source was found at Mungallala and a
bore drilled. The same line was provided with a staff member
known as a 'railway water pumper', who lived in a railway house
at Dulbydilla. In the 1930s, it was the railway water pumper's job
to pump water for the locomotives from the nearby creek. Once
a week, he would travel on the train to Angellala station where he
pumped water from the creek there into a large steel tank from
which the locomotives could draw.

The Woodline Trains

For the first fifty years of the twentieth century, there existed
around Kalgoorlie a giant web of light railway operations known
as 'the woodlines'. Millions upon millions of tonnes of wood were
cut and transported to the gold mines. In the days before electricity supply was widespread, steam was the prime source of power
at the mines; steam turbines provided the energy for the powerful
winders that operated the lifts in the mine shafts and for electric
lighting. That meant lots of wood (which was also needed for
props in the underground workings). The mine owners were the
beneficiaries of one of nature's riches: the acacia, or mulga, trees
that were found in profusion around Kalgoorlie. By 1900, the
mines were consuming 12,000 tons a day of this wood.

The West Australian Goldfields Firewood Supply Company
was the first in the business. It was soon followed by the Westralia
Timber and Firewood Supply Company which was to lay about
200 km of track. There were others: the Lakewood Firewood
Company maintained its own railway workshop and owned a

hotel, bakery, general store and butcher's shop at Kurrawang. The woodline trains from Kurrawang made round trips of 160 km, dropping off empty wagons at sidings and then collecting the filled ones on the return journey. Lakewood operated five trains a day at the height of the operation.

The firewood companies were not safe places at which to work. There were plenty of accidents during tree felling but the railways themselves accounted for a number of accidents and deaths. One gruesome end involved a shunter getting his foot caught in the rudimentary points as wagons were being propelled toward him.

But, after World War II, the days of these railways were numbered. Plentiful diesel and coal supplies were available via the government railway from Perth. The Lakewood company tried to keep going by converting to diesel locomotives but not only was the demand for wood declining but the remaining stands were becoming further and further away. The last wood train ran on 22 December 1964, with the rolling stock and track being sold for scrap.

The Radio Station Carriage

Jack Young of Ballarat, Victoria, had in 1931 obtained a licence from the state government to operate a mobile radio station anywhere in Victoria, so long as was not on the air within a 48.25 km (thirty miles) radius of an existing broadcasting station. His plan was to bring radio to country areas that could not normally receive good quality signals. He took the call-sign 3YB (today it is used by a commercial station in Warrnambool). His plan was to stay a week in any town, selling advertising and entertaining the locals — and then move on.

In mid-1932 Young leased a railway carriage built in 1899 to accommodate the Duke and Duchess of York (later King George V and Queen Mary) on their visit to Victoria. Victorian Railways charged Young £12 a week, a charge which included haulage between locations. The former royal parlour became the studio, complete with two turntables, a microphone and a library of one thousand records. What had been the royal dining area was used to house the transmitter. The remainder of the space was taken up by bedding for the crew. The station had a petrol motor for use when it could not hook into electricity supplies. The carriage had two six-metre masts which could be collapsed when on the move.

Station 3YB travelled through most of Victoria's regional areas. The carriage would be shunted into a siding and then the staff would fan out over town and sell advertising. The station would broadcast for four hours in the evening, starting at 6.00 pm. Birthday greetings cost two shillings and sixpence. A commercial advertising spot cost three pounds; businesses could also sponsor programming slots ranging from fifteen minutes in length up to an hour. 3YB lasted until 1935; its service became increasingly redundant as country towns got their own radio stations.

10

Ghost Lines, Vanished Places

NO LONGER CAN YOU get off a passenger train at Wodonga in northern Victoria and wait for the branch line train to Tallangatta and Cudgewa, or transfer at Moe for the mixed train to Thorpdale, or have a quick beer in the pub at Byrock in northern New South Wales after the main line train to Bourke has dropped you off and departed and you have a little time before the railmotor leaves to run up the Brewarrina branch. No longer, if you are a farmer at Mairjimmy in the Riverina, can you take your wool clip or wheat to that local siding and leave the rest to the railway. The rails just don't go to any of those places, anymore.

No, today it is all inter-modal freight speeding from one large city to another, or bulk grain or coal moving to a port behind several powerful locomotives. If a railway is to survive in today's world, that railway needs to pay its way. There is no place — alas — in our modern world for the country passenger train, or indeed the country railway station or sidings serviced by a few branch goods trains each week.

Australia is, as a result, littered with railway ghosts. A rusting hand-operated crane might indicate where a station yard was once located. A short length of formation, sometimes even of track in place, will reveal that trains once ran along that ground. Loading banks have either been bulldozed or left to disappear under grass and weeds. Some sections of working railway have been preserved by historical or railfan groups, with preserved old steam locomotives and ancient carriages are brought out from time to time just to remind us how railways once were.

But it can never be the same again. All we can do now is look at the photographs, check old timetables or tap the memories of the diminishing number of people who can remember what it was really like.

*　　*　　*

Not every railway line was a good idea. The sometimes rash decisions to build lines, often at the behest of politicians hoping to impress their electorates, too often guaranteed that whatever railway project that was being promoted would become a ghost line of the future.

There were some extraordinary rail projects undertaken. These included lines built but never officially opened such as the Nowingi-Millewa South line in the dry Mallee lands of northwest Victoria. Then there was the expensive failure of the line from Robinvale in Victoria to a place called Lette in New South Wales, when Lette was nothing more than a signpost. On 29 June 1892, Victorian Railways opened a new branch line in Gippsland, from the junction at Koo Wee Rup to Strzelecki, a distance of 49.1 km. However, the final 8.5 km from the small station of Triholm to the terminus was used by trains for little more than eight years. The Yannathan-Triholm section closed in 1941 after nineteen years of use. The remainder of the branch was gone by 1959.

As late as 1967, South Australia decided to extend its north-eastern broad gauge network by extending the line from the existing terminus of Paringa to a place called Chowilla. But that was never opened.

Queensland laid 37 km of track westwards from Winton to a place called 23 Mile. That section was completed in 1916 but was never opened to traffic, being dismantled in 1931. But that was not the state's railway planners' only costly mistake. Until 1930, all traffic from Brisbane headed for New South Wales had first to move inland to Wallangarra, the only point at which the narrow gauge Queensland system met the standard gauge of its southern neighbour. Passengers and freight had travelled 358 km within Queensland before they even reached the break-of-gauge point.

The circuitous route chosen also served the growing centre of Warwick; by this route, the distance to Brisbane to Warwick was 255 km, far longer than a direct line would have involved. In 1911, the Queensland government approved a plan to remedy Warwick's plight by laying a new line off the Fassifern branch. This was to allow what was seen as a more direct route (they named it the *Via Recta*, the Roman term for 'straight road') between Brisbane and Warwick — which it never reached. It took five years for the initial 9.2 km to be completed as far as Kalbar, the only real town the new line would ever serve. The other 16.7 km to Mount Edwards opened in 1922. Railway writer J. Armstrong, recalling the line's history a decade after it closed in 1960, said the project was doomed to failure even before work on it began. There was not even any sign of a settlement at Mount Edwards. 'The terminus was a farce,' wrote Armstrong.

The Mulgowie branch in Queensland was not quite such a disaster, but it certainly would never have contributed to the bottom line for Queensland Railways. This line left the Brisbane-Toowoomba main line at Laidley, a point 82 km from the state capital. The branch was opened on 19 April 1911 and, from the start, saw only one train a week. That service left Ipswich at 12.00 pm each Thursday, reaching Laidley by 2.45 pm, thence Mulgowie at 3.45 pm (just under an hour being a generous allowance for a branch stretching just 11.4 km in length). By 1950, the average load was one passenger every three weeks. Freight loads averaged ninety tons a week in the early years but even by 1937 (before road transport became a full-blown competitor) the branch was down to moving an average of just thirty-eight tons a week.

Tasmania, too, had its brushes with railway mania: there was the Apsley branch, a 42 km line into the hills from Brighton Junction. In an extraordinary decision, the Tasmanian parliament passed an authorisation bill in 1885 that would have had the line being laid with light (30 lb) rails, and built on a proposed route that would have involved both steep grades and sharp curves — so sharp, in fact, that only four-wheeler wagons and the smallest locomotives would have been able to use it; the then standard locomotives and bogie carriages of Tasmanian Government Railways would not have been able to negotiate such a branch. Department pressure (and common sense, obviously) prevailed and the line was built with 40 lb rails and to minimum TGR standards — no more than 1 in 40 grades and minimum five chain (about 100 metres) curves — were adopted. The line was opened on 22 April 1891. It clearly did not do well in its early years because, in 1897, the railway department unsuccessfully recommended closure. All the stations along the line were located on the main road, there was a low density of cropping in the area, hence restricted amount of produce to be transported, and the line did not extend to Bothwell, the only town of consequence in the area.

* * *

Many an intriguing name was lost when small railway stations closed. The people in a small settlement on the line to Werris Creek in New South Wales could not have been too happy when their station opened in 1886 was named Terrible Vale — better Warragundi which it was known as from 1913 until closure in 1975. On the section between Murrurundi and Werris Creek a station called Doughboy Hollow was opened to traffic on 13 August 1877; by 1893, it had become Ardglen. Possum Power Tank was a wayside stop between Stockinbingal and Temora opened on 1 September 1893; by 1895, it was Springdale. And who can say if the people waiting for a train at Henty station in the Riverina would not have been happier if the government railway had stuck with the original name, Doodle Cooma? And how many Sydney commuters waiting for their suburban trains at Epping station realise when it opened it was called Field of Mars? At least Jasper's Brush, on the south coast line to Nowra, kept its name until the end.

Tasmania also underwent a name transformation. When the colony's government took over the Tasmanian Main Line Railway Company in 1890, it set about renaming many of the stations. Among the vanishing names were Risdon Road (it became New Town), O'Brien's Bridge (Glenorchy), Lower Jerusalem (Woodlands), Antill Ponds Post Office (Woodbury) and Snake Bends became Powranna.

* * *

The main cause of death for smaller country stations was the gradual abolition of LCL — less-than-carload — traffic. The economies of the modern railway era could not accommodate trains stopping at each country station to engage in time-consuming shunting of wagons, detaching some and hooking up others. Once shunting en route was abandoned, there was no point having the vast network of country stations with their sidings, good sheds and loading banks.

This was the kiss of death for the small intermediate stations. Once shunting along the main line routes ended, there was no longer any reason to keep the smaller stations open even on those lines. Australian National Railways began phasing out LCL traffic in South Australia in the mid-1980s. Everywhere, eventually, the trains stopped stopping.

However, the cities have not been immune to closures. The Rogans Hill line in Sydney's west disappeared as early as 1932 while the Royal National Park line was a more recent casualty, closing in 1991. And not too many Melburnians would be aware there was once an Inner Circle line which met its end in 1948; North Carlton station remained in use as a community centre, but North Fitzroy and Fitzroy stations have long gone. The route, opened in 1898, ran from Heidelberg to Clifton Hill, thence Collingwood (later renamed Victoria Park) where the train reversed direction, passing again through Clifton Hill, then on to North Fitzroy, North Carlton, Royal Park, Macauley Road, North Melbourne and terminating at Spencer Street.

Amiens, a reminder of the war to end all wars

The Amiens branch in southern Queensland was unusual in many respects, none less than in the naming of all its stations after First World War battles: Fleurbaix, Pozieres, Bullecourt, Passchendaele,

Bapaume, Messines and Amiens itself. This was appropriate in that the line was built primarily to serve the soldier settlements established from 1917 to provide returned men with land and a means to earn a living. The project was called a 'tramway' as the Legislative Council in Brisbane (the then upper house) would not pass an enabling railway bill. However, the Mining Act gave the government a way out: allowed for tramways to be approved by regulation. Notwithstanding its official designation, the line was built to Queensland Railway standards. As the line's main purpose was to serve soldier settlements, the Federal government provided the entire construction cost of £50,364 by way of a loan. It was a line built during an incredible thirty year period of feverish branch line construction in southern Queensland. It was roughly a contemporary of branches that ran to places like Maryvale, Injune, Haden, Dayboro, Mount Edwards, Mulgowie, Canungra, Cooyar, Cecil Plains, Bell and Glenmorgan — among others.

The "Amiens Branch (Pikedale Tramway)", as it was known, was opened 7 June 1920. The branch left the Main Southern Line at Cotton Vale roughly halfway between Warwick and Wallangarra. Several war-related station names plans had been entertained. The line's surveyor suggested battlefields from Gallipoli and Palestine as well as France, with one station to be called Mons St. Quentin. The soldier settler administration wanted the stations named after six Queensland winners of the Victoria Cross.

The line's primary purpose was to transport fruit and vegetables from the farms and orchards along its length but it was a sitting duck once roads and vehicles improved. The distance from Amiens to Brisbane via rail was 322km, 96.5km farther than by road. For all its failings, the line survived far beyond what might have been expected, closing on 28 February 1974.

Dajarra, bigger than Texas

The people who lived and worked in the small settlement of Dajarra, at the end of the 54 km line that at Duchess branched off the Townsville-Mount Isa route, always claimed that more head of cattle passed through there each year than at any of the big rail yards of Texas, especially Abilene. There were other Australian stations which served the great inland trails connecting the railway to vast cattle properties of the outback — Marree in South Australia, Alice Springs and, in Queensland, Winton and Quilpie — but none of these aspired to claim to be the busiest in the world.

Dajarra was the closest railhead to the Northern Territory in the days before Darwin was linked by rail to the southern states. The rail reached this small place on 16 April 1917 and it tapped the cattle traffic from the Barkly Tableland and points west as far as the East Kimberley. During the Second World War, yearly shipments reached 95,000 head — said to be about 20,000 head greater than Abilene, Texas, in its heyday. There could be up to five trains a day pulling out of Dajarra and headed for the coast. It was the road trains that killed the line once sealed roads were available. The line to Dajarra closed on 31 December 1993. One visitor in the 1950s was not impressed. Lex Shepherd, in his book *My Own Boss*, recorded: 'For a railhead that held the world record for the largest number of stock trucked in a twelve-month period (1956), the Dajarra railway yard was abominable. The gates into the main receiving yard were situated in such a position that it was necessary to yard the cattle into the town'. He recorded that cattle from the Northern Territory were not accustomed be being among people, they were difficult to handle and were startled by noises such as a locomotive whistle.

Injune branch, which ran out of steam

This branch, which ran from Roma in central Queensland on the Western line, to the small town of Injune, was built, as so often, for the wrong reasons. The first 48 km of track to Orallo was laid to satisfy the demands of farmers; the second 52.6 km section was motivated by the soldier settlement scheme, both projects being ill conceived. Even one of its major sources of traffic was not much use when it came to balancing the books: when a coal deposit was discovered and a small mine developed to provide coal for Queensland Railways' locomotives, no charge was levied on the traffic for obvious reasons. As soon as dieselisation subsumed steam, this mine was no longer needed and the line closed on 31 December 1966.

The branch had its genesis in a 1911, held under the shade of a tree, where eight Orallo farmers decided to do something about getting a railway line so their produce could be readily transported to market. They eventually got their wish, and the government allocated £95,788, or £3,278 a mile, for a line to Orallo after Queensland Railway Commissioner Charles Evans presented a report to Parliament recommending the line. The state government, however, did require that local bodies whose areas benefited from the line — the Roma Town Council, the Booringa and Bungil shire councils - agree to make up any losses incurred by Queensland Railways Department on the Orallo line. As local historian Judith Barclay notes, the budget allowed for 2,640 sleepers and 880 cubic yards of ballast per mile, five intermediate stations (they ended up opening ten) and all the terminus facilities at Orallo, as well as the cost of buying the land. The wayside stations — Ona Ona, Tineen, Minka, Euthulla, Nullawurt, Yingerbay, Kingull, Nareeten, Oogara, Eumina and Moorta — were each provided with a waiting shelter and a cream stand. Yingerbay station became very busy on race days being located beside a racecourse, and special trains were run from Roma on those occasions.

In 1916, just as the Orallo section was being completed, the state government decided to extend the line to what was then known as Injune Creek, this time to open up 444 square miles for soldier settlement. These settlements were, generally speaking, failures with the new farmers (some of whom had no previous experience on the land) usually being allocated insufficient land to make a go of it — and/or being given marginal land that would have taxed the most skilled of agriculturalists.

Anyway, the extension of the branch was opened to traffic on 30 June 1920. Another ten stations were added. As for Injune, what had been a tiny settlement with a small store became, within six years of the rail being opened, what was described as a prosperous town with a Church of England, a School of Arts, police station, post office and telephone exchange (with twenty-six subscribers), school, newsagency, two boarding houses and a stock and station agent.

But it was never big enough to justify its own rail line; in 1961, the census put the population at five hundred people. Injune was initially run by a stationmaster, but from 1927 a less expensive station mistress-cum-gatekeeper ran the station. The locals must have thought twice before they bought a ticket to go into Roma. A return from Injune set them back ten shillings in 1920, an enormous slice of average weekly earnings. Can anyone today imagine paying, say, a sixth of their weekly income for a trip from the farm to go shopping in a regional town?

Tweed Heads, holiday destination

When the branch line to Tweed Heads, on the Queensland-New South Wales border, closed on 30 June 1961, it was not just the usual local protests that were heard. Large numbers of people were still using the weekend trains there to get to and from their homes in Brisbane. After all, it was the opening of the railway on 14 September 1903 that had suddenly propelled the growth of the area as both a holiday destination and a weekend getaway for city folk.

It meant the transformation of Coolangatta from tiny rural town to seaside resort. It was possible for up to six passenger trains a day to be scheduled to run into Tweed Heads at busy holiday times up until the late 1940s. Even as late as 1958, there could be four or more movements a day into Tweed Heads.

The Tweed Heads railhead was unusual in that it was the only Queensland railway station located outside the state, albeit barely, but definitely a few score metres inside New South Wales. So close was the border, in fact, that if locomotives reversed to the Coolangatta triangle for turning purposes, they were back across the border into Queensland within a few minutes.

Once the line was opened, hotels and guesthouses were thrown up at Coolangatta to accommodate the people flocking in from Brisbane. More stations opened as the region grew. Three were added in the short section inland from the beaches north of Coolangatta.

While the line depended on passengers for much of its revenue, there was a steady business in freight, too. Mineral sands, bananas and general goods were hauled out of Tweed Heads; there was also a fish shed where the local catch was stored until train departure time, and rail tankers brought oil to be shunted on to City Electric Light's power station siding. Fruit was also picked up at Currumbin and Mudgeeraba.

Mass car ownership spelled the end of the line; the latter-day passenger services were down to a locomotive and a handful of carriages. A competing bus service from Southport had also cut

Tweed Heads 1908, with a horse-drawn cart backed up to one of the
freight wagons. The advertisment on the fence is for a brand of schnappes.
Tweed Heads Historical Society.

into the railway's business. Business people mounted a campaign
to have the railway removed from the town centre and terminate
on the Queensland side of the border to free up traffic flow in the
business district; they ended up with more than they bargained for,
with the line being closed altogether.

Yaraka, a recent ghost

Life at Yaraka in central Queensland long revolved around the
weekly train. The town was connected to the world by its branch
line (and an unsealed road); the rail tracks covered the 271 km
gap from the junction of the Central Railway at Jericho. If you

are talking about the closest significant town, that is probably Emerald, 499 km from Yaraka. Rockhampton, the big smoke, is all of 767 km down the line. And the stations on the Yaraka line were far apart: Emmett, the closest to Yaraka, was 52 km from the terminus.

It all came to an end on 14 October 2005 when train No. 6373 pulled out of Yaraka for the last time. Brisbane's *Courier-Mail* newspaper, reporting on that last trip, noted that any trains in recent times had little more freight to haul than could have been fitted on a small truck. Local identity Elizabeth Ross told a gathering to farewell the final train that she had seen one recent working with the locomotive hauling a single wagon. The Yaraka line had become too expensive a proposition for Queensland Railways: the return trip from Alpha took more than eighteen hours, which meant sending two crews and coupling a van to the train so that the off-duty driver could sleep. The line was losing $4.5 million a year, and that money was to be diverted to the cost of sealing the road.

For decades, the Yaraka Mixed arrived on Wednesday evenings having loaded perishables at Rockhampton on late Tuesday morning. A refrigerated van, with a central partition separating frozen from chilled foods, was attached. The local general store would open Thursday morning with stocks of fresh milk and vegetables along with frozen food and fresh meat.

The absence of a sealed road saved the Yaraka passenger service after those on other, similarly trafficked lines had long gone. In 1989, Queensland Railways ordered the end of all passenger accommodation on all other branch line goods trains, but it was still possible after that to catch a train to Yaraka. Then, in 2001, the passenger car finally got the axe, and so a guard was no longer needed.

Kerry Whitfield had ridden the Yaraka Mixed in 1999. He boarded at Emerald for a 12.50am departure on one Wednesday morning. He found three long seats in the passenger compartment of the TGV van which each were long enough to stretch out for a sleep. There was a small table to prepare any food taken along; there was no water available, so passengers had to remember to take their own.

Brewarrina

It was wool that made the Brewarrina line what it was. This 93.7 km branch left the old Main Western line (that itself ran 803.6 km from Sydney to Bourke) at Byrock. Before the horrific drought that started in 1895 and lasted until 1903, more than one million sheep were farmed within Brewarrina's catchment area; even as late as the 1970s, around 20,000 bales of wool a year were consigned from Brewarrina railway station. Almost right up to its closure (after the floods of June 1974 caused serious damage to the line) a wool porter was employed at Brewarrina station; the bales of fleece came into goods shed spread over most of the year as various stations chose to shear at different times. Trains began running on 2 September 1901. Brewarrina station had a thirty metre-long platform, a goods shed, sheep and cattle loading yards, a turntable and weighbridge. In the early days, most of the town would be out to greet the train when it arrived from Byrock; then the crowd would move down Bourke Street to the post office and wait for the mail to be sorted.

When the line was disrupted by the flooding in 1974, the Brewarrina Shire offered to spend $10,000 to repair the railway to a standard where it could be used by goods and stock trains, if not passenger ones. The railways department rejected this proposal. Bus services began in September from Dubbo. Now, little sign remains of the railway: fire destroyed the station building in 1981, and the goods shed and turntable were removed in 1985.

Brewarrina, probably taken on opening day 2 September 1901, judging by the number of distinguished gentlemen posing on the platform for the camera, the carriages having been pulled away from the station verandah to help the photographer. The trailing carriage is a clerestory-roofed suburban car dating from the 1870s or 1880s. Paddy Norton Collection.

Finley, and the Tocumwal line

The 180.4 km Tocumwal branch has been out of action since 1988. In recent years, there has been local agitation to re-open it — after all, most of the infrastructure is in place (mainly the rails and the formation). This campaign was heartened by Victoria's decision to convert from broad to standard gauge its line which crosses the Murray River and which meets the end of the NSW rails. That, it seemed, would eliminate the difficulty which had hobbled the Tocumwal line, the break of gauge having been at that station.

Nothing changes in state rivalry; just as the colonial governments in New South Wales pushed railway lines into the Riverina in the nineteenth century to thwart Victoria's river and railway trade, the Tocumwal line remains firmly closed lest the southerners gain advantage in the twenty-first century.

Finley was, at one time, considered the largest depot in New South Wales for the transport of red gum railway sleepers. From the 1930s until into the 1950s, loads of sleepers from the Edwards River forest were delivered to the station for state-wide distribution. Inspection officers from the railways department would be in Finley once a month as part of the process of grading and branding the sleepers and ensuring payment to the cutters. Those sleepers rejected by the railways were eagerly bought by local farmers who used them as part of pig and poultry pens and for laying floors in loose boxes.

The railway was part and parcel of life to the people of Finley. In the 1930s and 1940s, married couples would frequently end up at the station on their big day to board a train for the honeymoon, usually to travel south to various Victorian destinations. The opening in the early 1920s of the Hay War Memorial High School provided secondary education for the children of the Riverina. Doug Donaldson, who has collected much of the line's history, remembers the trips home at the end of term when he was away at boarding school. A special train would leave Hay in the morning and reach Narrandera that afternoon. Children travelling for mid-year breaks would be billeted overnight with members of the Mothers Hospitality Club, a group comprising wives of local businessmen and clergy, before continuing their journeys home on another train. But at the end of the school year, the children would wait at Narrandera station for the southbound goods train leaving at 11.00 pm for Tocumwal. It was known as the 'midnight horror' to a generation of young students. They would sit in the guard's van as the train made its slow way down the Tocumwal line, the last of the students getting to their destination about 3.30 am. Donaldson remembers one trip home, in December 1930, when the 'midnight horror' could not get moving after its stop at Corobimilla. The problem: a plague of grasshoppers. The insects fouled the track so that the during which the locomotive could not gain traction on the rails. He recalls he and his fellow students helping the guard and fireman shovel cinders from the locomotive firebox on to the rails to get rid of the grasshoppers.

Milson's Point, by the sea

Before the Sydney Harbour Bridge opened on 3 March 1932, Milson's Point (the apostrophe was used then) was one of the busiest stations in New South Wales. It was there that the North Shore railway and tramway lines ended at the northern side of Sydney harbour. The city's main business district and government centre lay on the other side. Each morning hordes of people poured off the trains and trams to catch the ferries for the last part of the journey to work. In the evening, the trams and trains were waiting at Milson's Point as people who lived on the north side of the harbour teamed off the ferries. The noted railway historian, C. C. Singleton, who had witnessed much of the railway scene in the early part of the twentieth century, recorded the scene at Milson's Point in the days before the bridge:

> In the evening peak hour, crowded ferry steamers came storming alongside the pontoon with engines going full-astern and

churning the water noisily, the sponson bands screeching on the pontoon piles, the clanging of the engine room telegraph, the deckhands scurrying to make fast, the thumping of the feet of many impatient passengers jumping from the bulwark rail to the pontoon deck, the deckhands shouting 'Stand back' And 'Mind your feet, please', the running out of the clattering gangplanks and the shuffling feet of the disembarking passengers mingling with the background strains of 'Blind Billy' on his portable harmonium — all serving to create a pandemonium of sound peculiarly associated with that site. The arriving crowds divided into two streams — to the trains and to the trams ... Railway travellers without tickets crowded excitedly round the booking office window, usually missing trains that waited for nobody, though the more experienced 'old' hands purchased their tickets at the bookstall on the wharf at the Circular Quay end. Small boys hung about the platform in the hope of seeing porters operating the small lever frames for the crossovers to the middle road when releasing engines from the dead-ends.

Nimmitabel, gateway to the South Coast

Nimmitabel, as a town, never amounted to much in its own right. But it was located at a strategic point on the New South Wales rail line that pushed its way as far Bombala toward the southern Alps. The station opened on 20 April 1912 as Nimmitybelle, being changed to its permanent name the following October. Its importance derived from the fact that several much larger places between it and the coast, primarily the dairy processing town of Bega 77 km away, were not served by rail. Nimmitabel was the closest station to Bega. Large consignments arrived by train to be unloaded at Nimmitabel, not only for Bega but destined for other places along the coast including Bemboka. Coal also arrived by rail for transfer to Bega's gasworks — the town had, in 1885, been the first in New South Wales to open a municipal gasworks.

And the trucks came back carrying all the rural produce for railing to Sydney and other cities — butter from the dairy factories at Bega, Bemboka and Cobargo. When the wool clip was ready to be railed, the rail yards and surrounding areas were filled with trucks bringing in the bales. In a good season, four or five thousand bales of wool would be loaded at Nimmitabel. Livestock was big business, too. All the large properties sent cattle and sheep to the sales at Flemington markets in Sydney. Saturday was usually the busiest day for the loading of stock trains; the animals had been sold on the previous Monday at the Bega saleyards and then brought by drovers to the rail. At the busiest time of the year, there were also special trains run on Sundays. The fertiliser for the farmers in the district came in on railway wagons and its transfer to lorries was another manual task for the staff at Nimmitabel, which could number up to fifteen at a time.

The stock trains normally started at Bombala, picking up wagons from intermediate stations and — at Cooma — having a second locomotive added to the train. Drought also put pressure on the railway staff at Nimmitabel. In May 1968, it was decided to move large numbers of sheep from almost one end of New South Wales to the other. The wagons, once loaded, were moved in several sections to Cooma, where they were consolidated into one long train carrying 7,500 sheep. The *Cooma Express* newspaper reported that the train which pulled out of that town on 24 May was one of the longest ever to be seen in the Monaro region.

Special permission had to be obtained from the Railway Department's Engineering branch to run the train because of its size. Two 44-class engines are being used to pull it. These engines, the largest in the state, are rarely seen at Cooma. They are generally reserved for the Southern Aurora and other mainline expresses and were brought from Goulburn yesterday. A Railway Department Travelling Inspector is with the train which is expected to reach Burren Junction about 6pm tonight [the 25th May] … Most of the sheep were loaded at Nimmitabel but some were also collected at Jincumbilly, between Nimmitabel and Bombala.

Pattrick Buckley worked as a porter at Nimmitabel from 1954 until 1962, his days spent in the goods shed. There was no shortage of work. All the coal for Bega dairy factory came in by rail, each S-class wagon carrying between twelve and fifteen tonnes of coal — all of which had to be shovelled by hand into lorries for the rest of its journey by road. The mixed train to Cooma came through four mornings a week. The porters unloaded all the parcels and other consignments (from car parts to clothing) on to the platform from the guard's van for the waiting delivery trucks ready to speed their way to the shops of Bega and other places.

Nancy Burke arrived in Nimmitabel in 1942 when her father, Pat Doggett, was appointed stationmaster. After living at two remote stations along the Broken Hill line — Ivanhoe and Euabalong West — the Doggett family found Nimmitabel to be quite a change. Nancy remembers its snowing on the family's first Christmas at their new post.

The Nimmitabel railway station was busy, as the freight for Bega and the coast was brought here, to transport to Sydney and interstate. I remember some of the carriers Hayes and Kidd, Inskip and Thornton; the mail carriers, Hartley Sturah and Ray Lawler. A special treat was to miss a day's school and go with Dad to Bega on the mail truck, or with Mum (Maud) to Bombala on the train. Cooma was never in our area of travel, as we didn't own a car. I can remember when there were special trains run for butchers and bakers and railway men's picnics; and, when newlyweds went by train, Dad always put detonators on the line.

The railway south of Cooma's stockyards was closed on 26 March 1986, and Nimmitabel's seventy-four years as a busy rail centre were over.

Cudgewa, that most fascinating branch line

In its ninety or so years in existence, the Victorian branch line from Wodonga to Cudgewa achieved several distinctions. In that lifetime, the line had to be deviated nine times due to the building and then extension of the Hume Weir; one of its stations, Shelley, was the highest on the Victorian system at 781 metres; the branch played an important role in the construction of the Snowy Mountains Hydro scheme; finally, it was possibly the most picturesque of Victorian lines.

The branch, 113.5 km in total, skirted the southern banks of the Mitta Mitta River. Even the station names on this line suggested something out of the ordinary, Bandolier, Bandiana, Beetomba and Bullioh among them. Cudgewa never amounted to much as a town but its rail terminus was important; at one time, it was the third largest loading point for livestock on Victorian Railways. In steam days, it was common for stock trains to be assembled in two halves at Cudgewa, with the locomotive hauling one section up the heavy grade to Shelley and then returning light to the terminus to collect the other half of its train.

During the construction of the Snowy Mountains hydro-electric project, there were three goods trains a day arriving with construction materials; Thiess, the main contractor, had a lengthy siding at Cudgewa. In 1942, a third rail was laid 4.6 km along the line at the Wodonga end so that standard gauge trains from NSW could run into the then huge Bandiana army base, and later standard and broad gauge marshalling yards were built alongside each other. A migrant camp was also located along the branch at Bonegilla.

In the early 1950s, it was decided to increase the capacity of the weir and this forced Victorian Railways to put in place seven deviations between Bonegilla and Bullioh, which came into use on 24 July 1958. Huon Lane's large good shed was moved to the new site. It was one of the busier stations on the branch, its extensive trucking yards servicing the transport needs of farmers in what was a large and rich farming district. Shelley was also a busy station, with timber, livestock, skins and wool, railed from there.

But it was the army, Australia's post-war immigration policy and the Snowy Mountains hydro-electric scheme that, between them, kept the Cudgewa line operating as long as it did. The last train ran on 21 April 1978, while the line was officially closed on 1 March 1981.

The necessity of moving Australian military installations away from the coast in the Second World War meant that Bandiana became an important military establishment. Another military siding was opened at Bandolier; it, too, was a dual gauge siding to allow both NSW and Victorian rolling stock to run into the yards. Further along the line, Bonegilla served an army hospital, barracks and bomb disposal school. Bonegilla was to become even busier when, in 1947, the Immigration Department opened the Bonegilla Migrant Reception area. In the twenty-four years it operated (until 1971), more than 320,000 migrants passed through the centre.

Then, after the war, came the Snowy Mountains scheme which involved the damming of the great Snowy River to provide much needed electricity for eastern Australia. In the 1950s, Victorian Railways upgraded the branch: bridges were strengthened and ballasting was upgraded. At the Cudgewa terminus, the station building was moved and the yard enlarged to make room for a large Snowy Mountains Authority gantry crane to be erected for the unloading of steel, while another siding handled shipments of bulk cement. These heavy trains placed a considerable strain on the track — even with all the upgrading — and derailments were frequent.

The Mallee lines

Looking at a map of Victoria, you can understand the lure of the Mallee: for the purposes of this book, the region will be seen as defined by its railways — a vast rectangle, bordered to the west by the South Australian border; to the north by the Murray River; and to the south by an imaginary line running from Pinnaroo on the border to Ouyen. To the east, the border — and the *raison d'etre* for all that was to follow — was the railway line, completed to Mildura by 27 October 1903. The lessons of trying to farm those parts of Australia in which rainfall was unpredictable, to say the best, had yet to be fully learned.

The opening of that line to Mildura made possible the three railways that were to forge westward into the Mallee. The Mallee was, like so many other unsettled parts of Australia, an itch that had to be scratched. Nothing could halt attempts at settlement, and with more and more public and private money squandered. Of the three east-west lines in the Mallee, the Ouyen to Pinnaroo one was the last survivor. This railway had a reasonably robust life, and will concern us no further. Rather, the focus will be on the two routes that, without doubt, qualify as ghost lines: the 97 km railway from Red Cliffs to Morkalla that was completed by 1931 and was finally out of business in 1988; and the 39.1 km of track that ran from Nowingi to a place called 24 Miles. This last line was laid in 1929-30, never officially opened, but lingered on until the last rails were lifted in 1988.

A royal commission in 1911 reported that the Mallee land, running southwards from the Murray, was ideal for wheat growing and by 1921 the area was being considered for soldier settlement. And that would mean building a railway to allow the new farmers to transport their crops. When the surveyors set to work, they had a blank canvas. There were no towns, few roads. They could decide their route and, once that was decided, settlement would, of necessity, take place along either side of the railway line.

The first, but disregarded sign, of the problems that ahead for any settlers was that the state government was required to provide water tanks each holding 136,000 litres as the railway progressed, there being no surface water available. By April 1923, construction branch trains were operating over a 30 km section, with stations opened at Thurla, Benetook and Taparoo. The traffic included wagons with 9,000 litre tanks to provide water for the construction gang — which, by this stage, had forged rails through dense Mallee bush and sand hills. These men worked with horses and scoops, ploughs and rollers to tame the land.

Another sign of the difficulties ahead was the scene at Werrimull, the station which signified the end of the first section to be officially opened. When the station opened for business on 11 April 1924, there was a station all right — but not much else. It had a crossing loop and a 362 metre siding, but there was no sign of other human activity because the land was yet to be opened up for settlement. The clearing in which the station yard was located was surrounded by Mallee bush on both sides. The first (and official) train ran to Werrimull on 20 April 1924. Behind DD 689 were two 9,000 litre water tank wagons, a 3AB carriage and a Z guard's van. By October the following year, the extension to Meringur was completed, with the line's first reversing triangle installed, so eliminating locomotives having to run tender first back to Mildura.

However this did not sate the appetite for further lengthening of the line, and by 1927 there was talk of taking the rails to the South Australian border, possibly to link up with that state's Peebinga line. The immediate goal, though, was to build as far as Morkalla, and thus open up more land. Construction began in June 1930 and confidence was high that Morkalla would become a town of note. Yet when that latest section of line was opened there was need for only one mixed train a month — on the first Thursday of the month. The railway was soon dubbed the 'Once-a-Month line' by Melbourne's morning newspaper, *The Argus*. However, it was not until 1955 that any consideration was given to putting the Meringur-Morkalla section out of its misery. The last scheduled goods train ran to Morkalla on 2 June 1959 but the track was left in case it needed to be used for wheat specials at harvest time; it was officially closed to all traffic from 19 March 1964. Surprisingly, it was not until 1980 that Victorian Railways called for tenders to remove this extension, there having been sporadic campaigns to have the line rebuilt and re-opened during the intervening years.

Soon, the writing was on the wall for the surviving section of the railway. From 1972, it was decided to have the line open only part of the year, there being little traffic offering outside the wheat season. The main problem was that the line itself had not kept pace with advances in rolling stock, and the track could not cope with bogie wagons travelling at other than very slow speeds. In 1986 the decision was taken in Melbourne to keep running trains out to Meringur so long as it was safe to do so; as soon as there was concern about train safety on the line, the branch would be closed. That day came on 9 December 1988, By February 1991 the rails had been lifted and this Mallee line was just a footnote in railway history.

But the line was a blazing success by the standards of a project to its south. The claims were similar. A million acres would be opened by a railway and there were eight hundred British migrants expected to take up land were it offered, and the Commonwealth Government could be expected to provide finance under its development and migration policies. Then the director of soldier settlement argued that a 90 km line branching off the Mildura route at Nowingi would open up land for 16 km either side of the proposed branch. In December 1927 the Victorian Parliament passed the Nowingi to Millewa South Railway Construction Act, and another railway folly was unleashed.

An initial £35,000 was allocated in 1928 to get the work started. And by July 1929, some one hundred and six men were employed on building the new railway line. By the time it had penetrated 24 km into the Mallee, a businessman had applied for a siding to be built for the loading of gypsum, a mineral found in substantial quantities in the area. But the railway project was facing problems. One was lack of water, with large quantities having to be carted along the to the work camp; another was the discovery that the site of one proposed station along the line lay at a spot where there was already a large sand ridge.

A new state government viewed the project as a calamity; this was just three months after the line (uncompleted) saw its only ever steam locomotive hauled passenger train in the form of the special working to carry Chief Commissioner for Railways Harold Clapp on an inspection visit. Work was suspended in late 1929 when the money ran out. In 1941, the Victorian parliament was asked to approve legislation enabling track beyond the 18 mile point to be dismantled. By the time the railway had been completed, £83,803 had been spent. By that time, too, sand drifts were becoming a problem, with large deposits left across the track when the winds blew.

A postscript to this unusual 'ghost' train is that, while the line was obviously in use in the 1930s, it remained under the construction branch as an unfinished project. It was later acknowledged as a Victorian Railways route that opened officially on 12 May 1942.

Bellerive-Sorell - a sorry story

No wonder that, at £9,000 a mile, the Bellerive to Sorell railway became one of the most expensive pieces of railway construction in Tasmania. Bellerive is located on the banks of the estuary of the River Derwent opposite the city centre of Hobart, and the 23.6 km line was intended to provide transport for farmers of Sorell, then the granary of the island, to Bellerive whence their produce could be moved across the estuary by ferry.

Even without the cost of a bridge across the Derwent, the chosen route for the line required a railway pier at Bellerive, 256 metre-long bridge across Pittwater, a 582 metre viaduct and a 164 metre tunnel. And that was without the various cuttings that had to be chiselled through hard sandstone.

In addition, the fact of it being an isolated railway meant that every rail, every piece of timber, and certainly every locomotive, wagon and carriage, had to be transported by boat to Bellerive; then at Bellerive there had to be large goods shed and, along the line, a weir with a capacity of two million litres for watering the locomotives — and there also had to be capacity to handle and store the coal for those locomotives, coal which had to be shipped from Newcastle in New South Wales. Its isolation certainly condemned the line to an earlier death than would have been the case if it had been connected to the main Tasmanian network. The Bellerive to Sorell railway opened on 2 May 1892; just thirty-four years later, as of 30 June 1926, it was dead.

Because of its isolated status, the Bellerive-Sorell line needed a rolling stock fleet to cover all eventualities: four first class and four second class carriages, two brake vans and forty-seven wagons including open (low, medium and high sided) and covered ones, two horse boxes (transporting race horses to the course at Sorell was a useful source of income for the line) and livestock wagons. Trains carried grain, chaff, wood, wool and cream. A third locomotive was added later as were more carriages and brake vans and — an indication of the popularity of the races — three more horse boxes.

The carriages were not fitted with Westinghouse brakes, an extraordinary situation to persist into a twentieth century on a government railway. Nor, according to a newspaper report at the time of the closure, had they been painted during their thirty-three years of service running between Bellerive and Sorell — and they were not exactly new items of rolling stock when there were brought across the Derwent in 1892. The carriage fleet on this isolated section was equipped with four-wheeler cars with seating running longways beneath the windows. They had been built between 1875 and 1885 for the Tasmanian Main Line Railway Company.

There was only one piece of equipment missing: they never got around to laying sets of rails on the ferry so that wagons could be taken across the river rather than freight having to be handled between rail wagons and ferry at Bellerive, a factor that added to costs and meant delays in transhipments. The railway's downfall was due, essentially, to the fact that it did not provide the speed of service that the farmers required. Produce could lie in the yards at Bellerive for two or three days before being loaded on the ferry. That, and the fact that the line was a severe drain on the railway budget, losing money every year except one (1902), this situation worsening as road transport improved.

By 1925, the two daily trains each way had become one return service and the department's report noted that only a small amount of traffic was being consigned to the railway. An engineer's report stated that the line would need repairs to the tune of £10,000 and that the railway would need new rolling stock. The end came on 30 June 1926, vociferous local protests notwithstanding. The line was closed with little ceremony. Hobart's *The Mercury* newspaper reported that only two old men and the stationmaster were there at 4.40pm to witness the last scheduled departure from Bellerive, consisting of five carriages and two wagons. "Not a cheer was raised; not even a dog howled," the newspaper noted.

Zeehan, remote rail centre

Zeehan was, in the heyday of mining on Tasmania's west coast, the third largest town on the island with more than 10,000 people living there. It was quite a rail centre: at its zenith, the station handled a greater freight tonnage than any Tasmanian station with the exception of Hobart and, at one time, accounted for almost thirty per cent of freight carried by Tasmanian Government Railways — not entirely surprising considering that the various railways and tramways radiating from the town served four smelters. All these needed constant supply of ore; moreover, coal and coke had to be hauled from the wharf at Strahan after being shipped from New South Wales. A single collier would deliver enough coal or coke to fill five trains.

Conservation of forests was not a priority when it came to forging railways through the bush. Here one of Tasmanian Government Railways locomotives pauses for the camera at Confidence Saddle near Zeehan at what was then the eight-and-a-half-mile mark. Archives Office of Tasmania.

Ore being loaded at the mine site on the North-East Dundas Tramway operated by Tasmanian Government Railways. This photograph gives a good view of the rolling stock used and emphasises the narrowness of the gauge chosen for this line. Archives Office of Tasmania.

Public holidays were also busy times for Zeehan station with up to two thousand people being moved to Macquarie Harbour for a day out. The railways of Zeehan consisted of an isolated section of Tasmanian Government Railways line (1,067 mm) and a number of mine and forestry lines, usually of 610 mm gauge, radiating from it into the rugged terrain that surrounds Zeehan.

In addition to TGR trains, those of the Emu Bay Railway Company had the running rights over 3.2 km of government line from Rayna Junction into Zeehan. In fact, the Emu Bay line eventually made the TGR section redundant; the government had built its line to provide mines with access to the nearest port, that being Strahan on Macquarie Harbour. But the Emu Bay line provided access to Burnie, a port on the northern coast of Tasmania that was nearer markets and also far safer in navigation terms; this was fatal for TGR's operations. When, on 4, June 1960, the last TGR train ran into Zeehan, the locomotive and brake van then ran up the Emu Plains track to rejoin the TGR system at Burnie.

The first 45 km section from Zeehan to Strahan was opened on 4 February 1892. When mines opened at Mt Dundas, a 12 km extension was built by the Dundas-Zeehan Railway Company with TGR trains operating over the new section. The Zeehan rail operation was very profitable in the early years with trains being fully laden in both directions — construction materials going one way, mined ore the other. On 16 October 1900 the line was further extended, this time at the Strahan end, with 1.6 km of new rails allowing government trains to run through to Regatta Point and there meet the seaboard terminal of the Mt Lyell Mining and Railway Company trains from Queenstown. An island platform was built to allow both operators to use the station simultaneously.

But it was only another two months until the Emu Bay line saw its final section, from Guildford to Rayna Junction, completed and that company obtain running runs over TGR's rails into Zeehan. Prior to that, all mineral output had been railed to ships at Strahan. But the opening of the Emu Bay line meant that almost all ore went up the line to Burnie. The shipments through Strahan had ended by 1908.

While TGR thereafter struggled with the economics of its operations, other lines sprang up. These included the Zeehan Tramway Company which from 1892 provided, with its 610 mm network stretching just 9.65 km in all, to provide transport for ore and the miners between Zeehan and mines, including British Queen, Florence and Mt Zeehan. The tramway carried coal, coke, machinery, ore and firewood. There was plenty of passenger traffic on offer, too: eleven passenger trams ran on weekdays, according to an 1893 timetable, starting at 8.00 am and the last one running at 6.00 pm. This service ended in 1905 although occasional passenger excursion trams operated after that year and almost up until closure. By 1919, all the mines had closed and the company's track became use for timber traffic.

TGR itself built a tramway; the government considered a full-scale heavy 1,067 mm line too costly for what was to become known as the North-East Dundas Tramway. The line would have cost more than £10,000 a mile if had been built to the existing Tasmanian government railway gauge. The cost of the Zeehan-Regatta Point section had been £8,058 a mile, including the cost of the rolling stock and the construction of a bridge at Strahan. So the two foot (610 mm) gauge with curves of not less than ninety-nine feet (30.2 metres) was adopted instead of the 1,067 mm. The line included many reverse and compound curves; the number of curves averaged thirty per mile. There were ten bridges (including one overbridge), and the ruling grade was 1 in 25.

The line became noted in Australian railway history because the first two Garratt locomotives ever built were ordered for this line. The Garratt was a then new concept where a common boiler was pivoted between two separate engine units which in turn delivered power two separate sets of driving wheels. Its articulated frames made the engine suitable for lines where there were tight curves. The two engines, numbered K1 and K2, were brought into service on the tramway in 1910 to haul the wagons of silver-lead concentrate.

The railway workshops at Launceston built twenty-five eight wheeled, low sided wagons each capable of carrying ten ton for the tramways; in addition, it constructed six eight wheeled flat wagons; two four wheeled bolster wagons for carrying long pieces of timber; and four passenger cars, each fitted with six cross seats with reversible backs, enough to seat eighteen passengers in each car, along with lockers for mail and parcels. Apart from mine production coming out along the tramway, the TGR used this line to cart huge quantities of firewood in the other direction to provide fuel for the mining operations. The last train on the main tramway route ran on 5 July 1932. With the closing of the Comstock line in 1933 came the end of the 610 mm system at Zeehan.

The Zeehan-Strahan line operated by TGR was also badly hit by the Great Depression; most of the rolling stock was moved to the main government system in the east and north of Tasmania. The last train from Regatta Point in 1960 was an apt reminder of the line's decline: it comprised just V-class diesel No. 9, a stock wagon, a box wagon and an open wagon, along with composite brake van DB14 which had been built in 1886. TGR left behind two of its FFF wagons for a timber company that, for some years, continued to use 8 km of the government line with steam locomotive C1 as its tractive power.

Port Adelaide, back then

Trains still run into Port Adelaide. Containers are moved there, so is wheat. And trains run to Outer Harbour where Adelaide's shipping action now takes place. So, Port Adelaide has not vanished;

but it has changed. No longer is it a place where, as Gifford Eardley wrote in 1970:

> There is a fascination about railway tracks which nose in and out of wool and produce stores, diving into various doorways by means of tiny turntables and circumnavigating the sur-rounds of small shipping basins and wharf-lined docks. The maze of tracks at old-time Port Adelaide formed by far the most complex system that served any of the Australian ports and, strangely enough, the largest as far as the nineteenth century was concerned.

This was a time when windjammers carried out South Australia's wheat, wool and copper. Then there were schooners and small sailing ships that traded with Tasmania; others brought coal from Newcastle.

The colony's government chose Port Adelaide as the terminus of the first railway built out of Adelaide itself. The broad gauge (1,600 mm) track, 11.5 km in length, was opened on 21 April 1856. In the following year, a siding extension was laid across St Vincent Street and then along Lipson Street on to McLaren Wharf.

Here it was that locomotives and other rolling stock being imported were unloaded as the South Australian rail network expanded. South Australian Railways locomotives were used on the wharf on these occasions, but initial traffic with other freight saw wagons hauled by horse teams. Extraordinary though it seems, horses continued to pull rail wagons at Port Adelaide until the 1920s. So familiar did the horses become with the rail operations, Eardley reported, that they would — without needing any com-mand — as they approached a other wagons on the line, move sideways away from the track to allow the loaded wagon to move past them. Teams of horses were everywhere to be seen, each wearing a white cap with holes for ears to keep the hot sun off their heads. For all the teams of horses, and the heavily congested sidings, there was very little shouting by teamsters; the horses knew what they were doing.

The crew on board 2-4-0 locomotive P 177 appears to be waiting for the yard shunters to do something — perhaps throw points or uncouple a wagon — as the photographer caught the scene in August 1954 at Port Dock yard, Port Adelaide. The broad gauge locomotive was built in 1893 and spent the bulk of its life hauling suburban passenger trains. P 117 is preserved at the National Railway Museum. D.A. Colquhoun collection—National Railway Museum.

If that was not enough to clog the streets, there were hundreds of road wagons, pulled by one horse or teams of four. As these and the rail lines shared the same roads, the drivers of the road vehicles had to be constantly on the alert so they did not become wedged between moving rail wagons. Eardley, who witnessed this era in the company of his grandfather, recalled the excitement 'with horses rearing and kicking out of their traces, whips cracking, shafts becoming entangled, and men screaming oaths which would make a bullock driver blush with shame'.

At the Prince's Wharf, there had been laid a maze of short loop sidings, points, crossovers, wagon-length shunting spurs, all hemmed into a small space by surrounding buildings. It was a muddle. Meanwhile, the railways department was receiving complaints because, due to the congestion at the Port Adelaide station itself, wagons were stored on the street branch lines in Lipson Street and Commercial Road. The single line to Adelaide meant that the route could not cope with all the traffic, so up to eight goods wagons were attached to every passenger train; in some cases there were as many as twenty wagons if the passenger train had only a few carriages. The problem was that the goods wagons did not have spring buffers, so that starting and braking meant a very uncomfortable time for passengers. Separate goods trains were run from 1870, and in 1880 the government decided to duplicate the line.

Narrogin, a railway crossroads

Today, long diesel-hauled trains roar through Narrogin in Western Australia. But nobody waits there to catch a train anymore. Yet it was quite a different scene forty or fifty years ago.

Maurie Dawson, who worked as a porter there, recalls that in the early 1960s there could be as many as seventeen trains go through Narrogin on a week night. He was rostered as night porter, and would wait for the express to arrive from Perth on its way to Albany. His job was to unload parcels destined not only for Narrogin but ones that had to reloaded into vans being hauled down the Collie, Corrigin and Kondinin branch lines. With the help of another porter he would handle enough parcels to make eight barrow loads. Their work that night would also include handling the milk churns that arrived on Train No. 103 from Collie, or the twenty or more bags of mail arriving aboard Train No. 46 from Corrigin.

A decade earlier, according to a local newspaper article published on 30 April 1953, Maurie would have been a great deal busier. This recorded that up to thirty-four trains a day were cleared through Narrogin, and 10,000 tons a day of goods loaded or unloaded. Three hundred and fifty people were employed by Western Australian Government Railways at Narrogin in 1953.

From 1926, trains could operate in five directions from Narrogin as it became the meeting point for cross-country and branch lines serving the farmers of the state. This inevitably led to a much larger station building, along with all the usual accoutrements of being an important junction: large marshalling yard, workshops and locomotive depot. A District Superintendent, District Traffic Superintendent, District Locomotive Super-intendent and a District Engineer, along with their staffs, were posted to the town.

A diagram of the station in 1987 shows an island platform with a footbridge spanning sidings to both east and west of the station building, sixteen roads in all. The 1956 working timetable reveals just how busy Narrogin was in a typical week. Goods trains departed from 12.50 am until 7.10 pm. There were daily services to Merredin via Corrigin (departing 4.00 am), Collie (5.40am and

10.00am) and, Mondays excepted, to Albany (2.41 am). Four days a week saw No. 24 Goods would leave at 6.30 am for York, No. 71 at 8.15 am for Katanning and No. 23 at 2.20 pm for the same destination. Katanning also had a Monday 12.50 am departure, a 4.10 pm train on Tuesday and Thursday and, on three days a week, a goods train leaving Narrogin at 7.00 pm. In addition, Mondays saw workings to Wagin (1.20 am), Kondinin (8.00 am) and Spencers Brook (7.10 pm). Wednesday was train day for No. 192 Fast Goods leaving at 6.00 am for Dwarda and Pinjarra and No. 154 Fast Goods for Spencers Brook (6.50 pm). Several other train services ran twice-weekly. This profile does not include all the fertiliser or wheat specials that ran to and through Narrogin.

Narrogin got its start because of its local water supply. Narrogin Pool was seen as a splendid source of water for locomotives. The fettler gangs pitched tents near the present station location, and businesses followed. In 1953 there was a stationmaster and four assistant stationmasters. The traffic branch included a chief clerk, transport officer, livestock clerk, four train inspectors, along with the guards, shunters, porters and other workers vital for a busy junction station. The refreshment room staff each morning had to wash the brown linoleum floor. After all, the trains passing through all night, and dirt being trampled in by passengers grabbing pies and tea while the expresses paused, meant a floor black with coal dust. The day's work also meant chopping wood to fuel the stoves in the kitchen. In the 1930s, 'Cocky' Vaughan was District Traffic Superintendent and would arrive at work at 4.00 am, upon which he would commence an inspection, running a finger over luggage racks to check for any dust. Jack Hastie, who worked at the station back in the 1930s, recalled it was 'woe betide' the worker responsible if Vaughan found even a single match lying on the platform.

The platform would have seen many passengers milling about as people arrived from branch line trains and waited for the Perth and Albany expresses. Bill Craig, who was yard foreman in 1952, described a typical pre-Christmas shift at Narrogin where there were

> ... ducks, fowls, turkeys, geese being hastened to the slaughter; ham-shaped parcels being sent here and there; stone fruit, tomatoes, salads, etc. by the van-load, going out to all the outback places; tubs and tubs of ice cream; cases and cases of cool drink; barrels and barrels of beer — all in addition to the people travelling. Christmas is not an easy time on the railways.

Ravensthorpe, where the trains stopped for flower picking

When mining boomed at the location called Ravensthorpe in Western Australia, it was necessary to transport equipment and supplies in and the ore out through a nearby port, and that was Hopetoun on the western end of the Great Australian Bight. On 3 June 1909 the completed railway link, 54.4 km in all, was officially opened as a Western Australian Government Railways (WAGR) line. The following year the line's senior staff were moved to Ravensthorpe and that became headquarters of the isolated section under a District Stationmaster.

However, international copper prices collapsed in 1911 and the mine was closed; the railway headquarters were returned to Hopetoun. WAGR in 1914 decided to rehabilitate the mine and then leased it and the smelting plant to a private operator in order to starting generating freight revenues. But in 1919 mining stopped again. Thereafter, the local farmers provided some business but the volume was sparse. The passenger timetable allowed three hours for the train to cover the short length of the line; the trains would stop to allow passengers to shoot game and, in season, to pick wildflowers.

Excursion trains for the people of Ravensthorpe were operated throughout the 1920s as the railway had passenger carriages and the trains gave the settlers a day by the sea. From 1 April 1931, WAGR cancelled regular services and brought the line into operation only when grain had to be hauled out or superphosphate in; the attitude was to move the harvested grain and then close the line down again as quickly as possible until the next season. The line operated for only seven weeks in the whole of 1935. It closed that year, as of 23 February and never re-opened. Road transport saw it off.

Western Australia's Zigzag

New South Wales' zigzag railway built to allow trains to climb and ascend the inland side of the Blue Mountains has justly became world famous. At the other extreme, Mildura, Victoria, had a short, 1 km zigzag broad gauge branch line with two reversing stages to transfer stock from boats on the Murray River up to the main railway line. This branch was opened in September 1922 and closed on 20 March 1973.

But there was one other substantial example in Australia — at Kalamunda in Western Australia a zigzag was constructed to allow trains to ascend and descend the Darling Ranges. A three-stage zigzag was laid between Ridge Hill and Gooseberry Hill on what would become the 33.2 km Midland-Karragullen line (a fourth stage was added in 1912). The line's official title was the Upper Darling Range Railway after it came under government control, and it was extended from the then railhead at Canning Mills to its eventual terminus of Karragullen. The highest point on the line was 320 metres. The initial surveys revealed that the track would have to climb 305 metres, and the decision to construct a zigzag was made to avoid the high costs of tunnelling as well as avoiding the need to construct embankments and excavate cuttings.

The zigzag section provided that trains could climb or descend 129 metres in a distance of 6.1 km; the average grade was 1 in 38, although its maximum was 1 in 27. A private saw-milling company undertook the construction the line which came into use during July 1891 having been built in eleven months by the contractor Edward Vivian Keane. Soon after opening, the Canning Jarrah Timber Company bought both the timber concession and the railway. By the time of its completion, the timber mill at the top had stockpiled 70,000 jarrah railway sleepers for transporting by the new line.

The line became part of Western Australian Government Railways on 1 July 1903. There was no run-round at the top of the line, so the carriages had to be guided under their own gravity into a dead end on the zigzag which left the locomotive at the front end for the remaining descent. Passenger trains took two and a quarter hours to travel the line.

The end came when the national railway strike of 1949 disrupted all traffic, and the opportunity was taken by the state government to close the branch as of July 22 that year, although a short 1.6 km spur to a brickworks siding near the main line junction remained open until 1956. The branch had been losing money for years with road transport taking away both freight and passengers — until the 1940s, the roads there had been fairly rudimentary and the railway was the only effective means of travel or shifting goods. The following year saw the state government pass the Railways (Upper Darling Range) Discontinuance Act, the line was torn up and the zigzag sealed for the use of road traffic.

Today the zigzag route is promoted as a scenic drive offering views over the greater Perth area. Kalamunda itself is now considered an outer suburb of the state capital.

Walkaway — very English and a railway border

Walkway became an important railway post as of 1894. It was the station at which the Western Australian Government Railways line from Geraldton met the track owned by the Midland Railway Company which covered the 442.3 km to Midland Junction on the edge of Perth. The Midland company had been floated in London and brought with it the English style of station construction. Walkaway's station was built of stone with brick chimneys. The company eschewed the Australian practice of locating the stationmaster's house away from the station. Instead, it adopted the British system of having the stationmaster's home being located on the first floor of the station itself.

There was a refreshment room although, in later years, many passengers preferred to dash across the road to the local pub while the locomotives were being changed from one operator's to the other's. But by the late 1940s, most of the coaching stock was government equipment. Just south of the Walkaway station was a small village housing Midland staff, most of whom were employed at the locomotive depot there. There was a coal stage and the Midland company had built a large dam up in the hills (it is still there, although not in use). The village also housed the drivers, firemen, guards and fettlers. All gone today, of course, but the surviving station lives on as a reminder of the days when Walkaway stood out on the map as the border between two railway operators.

11

Vital Statistics

- The longest straight stretch of railway in Australia (and the world) is the 478 km section between Ooldea and Nurina on the transcontinental rail line. However, the idea that this line is just one long straight section is a popular misconception, largely due to the well-known photographs that show the line disappearing into the distance without any visible curvature. In fact, when the line was opened, there were 443 curves between Port Pirie in South Australia and Kalgoorlie in Western Australia. New South Wales did have one straight section 187 km long but that (between Nyngan and Bourke) is now closed to traffic. There is a 115 km straight section on the Darwin line; it begins 8 km north of Alice Springs.
- The highest point on Australian railways was at Ben Lomond, New South Wales, on the now closed section of the Main North line to Wallangarra, Queensland. That point was 1,370 metres above sea level.

- The longest railway bridge in Australia crosses the Coomera River in Queensland, and is 858 metres long. The line connects Brisbane with the Gold Coast.
- The highest railway bridge is the Sydney Harbour Bridge. Its two railway tracks connect the city with the North Shore line and reach 60 metres above the water's surface.
- The longest timber rail bridge in Queensland was the trestle at Angellala on the Western line. It was 643.5 metres long, although 84.7 metres of it was later rebuilt with steel.
- Australia's longest railway platform is the No. 1 platform at Flinders Street, Melbourne. It was built at 639 metres in length. The second longest is the 508 metre platform at Kalgoorlie, the third being the 460 metre-long platform at Albury, New South Wales.
- The longest tunnel in Australia (apart from city underground tunnels) is the Cox's Gap bore (1.93km) on the Sandy Hollow-Ulan coal line in New South Wales.

Worst accidents

Granville, New South Wales — 18 January 1977. A suburban Sydney electric train set derailed and struck an overhead bridge. The structure collapsed on top of the train. In all, eighty-three people died and another eighty passengers were injured.

Sunshine, Victoria — 20 April 1908. Forty-four people were killed and 431 injured when an Easter Monday special from Bendigo headed by two locomotives passed multiple stop signals and ran into the back of a passenger train from Ballarat which was standing at the platform of Sunshine station.

Murulla, New South Wales — 13 September 1936. A collision occurred after several wagons and a brake van became uncoupled from their train at this small station located in the Upper Hunter Valley. The wagons and van ran out of control down the grade and crashed into the oncoming Northwest Mail passenger train. Twenty-seven people were killed and forty-two injured.

Hawkesbury River, New South Wales — 20 January 1944. The Kempsey mail train struck a bus at the level crossing near Brooklyn station. It was reported that the gates were open and that the driver proceeded to cross the line without knowing a train was approaching. The bus was wrapped around the front of the locomotive and carried for a quarter of a mile (about 400 metres). All the fifteen dead — which included two nuns and two children from St Catherine's Orphanage — were on the bus.

Camp Mountain, Queensland — 5 May 1947. A train travelling at excessive speed derailed, killing sixteen of those on board and injuring another thirty-eight. The working was a special excursion train heading for Dayborough.

Exeter, New South Wales — 16 March 1914. The Temora Mail passed a stop signal and collided with a goods train reversing into the passing loop. Fourteen people were killed and thirty-two injured.

The most recent in the category of rail accidents occurred on 5 June 2007 when a semi-trailer collided at a level crossing near Kerang, Victoria, with a southbound V/Line passenger working. Eleven train passengers died.

Shunting a private sidings is becoming a thing of the past. Here in 1983, New South Wales locomotive 4878, its train left on the main line, picks up wagons from a dairy factory at Geringong on the state's south coast. Robin Bromby.

It was 11 October 1965 and Px 201 has arrived at Peebinga, the end of a South Australian branch into the Mallee near the Victorian border. Obscured by the wagon on the adjoining track is a passenger carriage. All mixed trains on this line ceased on 1 July 1973. J. Southwell—National Railway Museum.

Bibliography

Periodicals

Bulletin, Newsrail, Railway Digest, Railways in Australia, Tasmanian Railway News

Books

Adam-Smith, Patsy, *Romance of Australian Railways* (Rigby) 1973

Barclay, Judith, *A Thing of the Past: Roma to Injune by Train* (self-published) 1991

Barden W.D, *Mullewa Through the Years* (Mullewa Roads Board) 1961

Bayley, William A., *Border City: History of Albury NSW* (Albury City Council) 1954

Bromby, Robin, *Rails to the Top End* (Cromarty Press) 1982

Bromby, Robin, *The Country Railway in Australia* (Cromarty Press) 1983

Bromby, Robin (ed.), *Australian Railway Companion* (Sherborne Sutherland) 1989

Bunbury, Bill, *Timber for Gold: Life on the Goldfields* (Fremantle Arts Centre Press) 1997

Carroll, Brian, *Australian Railway Days: Milestones in Railway History* (Macmillan) 1976

Cooley, Thomas C.T., *Railroading in Tasmania* (Government Printer) 1964

Ferry, John, *Junee and the Great Southern Railway* (Junee Shire Council) 2001

Fitch, R.J., *Making Tracks* (Kangaroo Press) 1989

Fluck, R.E., Sampson R., and Bird, K.J., *Steam Locomotives and Railcars of the South Australian Railways* (Mile End Railway Museum) 1986

Gregory, J.W., *The Dead Heart of Australia* (John Murray) 1906

Herbert, Xavier, *Capricornia* (Publicist Publishing Co) 1938

Holmes, Lloyd, *The Branch Line: A History of the Wodonga-Tallangatta-Cudgewa Railway* (self-published) 1993

Holmes, Lloyd, *A Railway Life* (self-published) 1991

Houghton, John et al, *The Bellerive to Sorell Railway Revisited* (Bellerive Historical Society) 2005

Ireland, Frank, *Nimmitabel: A story of a town and its people* (self-published) 1993

Kerr, John, *Triumph of the Narrow Gauge* (Boolarong Publications) 1990

Maclean, Meta, *Drummond of the Far West* (Manly Daily) 1947

Messner, Andrew, *Train Up! Railway Refreshment Rooms in New South Wales* (Australian Railway Historical Society) 2003

Phillips, Joy (ed.), *Charleville Railway Centenary 1888-1988* (Charleville Railway Centenary Committee) 1988

Preston, R.G., *Day of the Goods Train* (Eveleigh Press) 1988

Smith, Keith, *Tales of a Railway Odyssey* (Railmac) 2001

Thomson, James, *Nor'West of West* (Gordon & Gotch) 1908

Twain, Mark, *Following the Equator: A Journey Around the World* (American Publishing Company) 1897

Photographs: State Records NSW, as part of its efforts to assist researchers of the future, require the inclusion of the following citation for pictures from its collection used in this book: SRNSW: Digital ID: 17420_a104_a01400082.

The author is grateful to all those who supplied photographs for inclusion in this book.

Other E-Books by Robin Bromby

German Raiders of the South Seas: The extraordinary true story of naval deception, daring and disguise, 1913-1917. The story of the German surface raiders *Emden*, *Wolf* and *Seeadler* in the Pacific and Indian oceans in the First World War. In 1914 Germany had a large presence in the Pacific — a naval base at Tsingtao, China, and colonies spread from Micronesia through New Guinea to Western Samoa, and a huge merchant shipping fleet. But all this was lost as soon as war began and made even more amazing the exploits of the three ships which independently waged war on Allied shipping. Apart from the astonishing number of victims they caught and sunk, this is a story of remarkable seamanship — whether it be the voyage of the *Emden* survivors to the Red Sea or the heroic sailing in an open boat by the *Seeadler's* captain.

The Farming of Australia: A saga of backbreaking toil and tenacity. From the first efforts of transported convicts, the new settlers in Australia forged an agricultural miracle in an island continent again pestilence, drought, distance and heartbreak.

If you wish to be advised of new Highgate titles, email to info@highgatepublishing.com.au

Printed in Great Britain
by Amazon